Acrylic Painting
Step-by-Step

WENDY JELBERT, DAVID HYDE
& CAROLE MASSEY

SEARCH PRESS

Contents

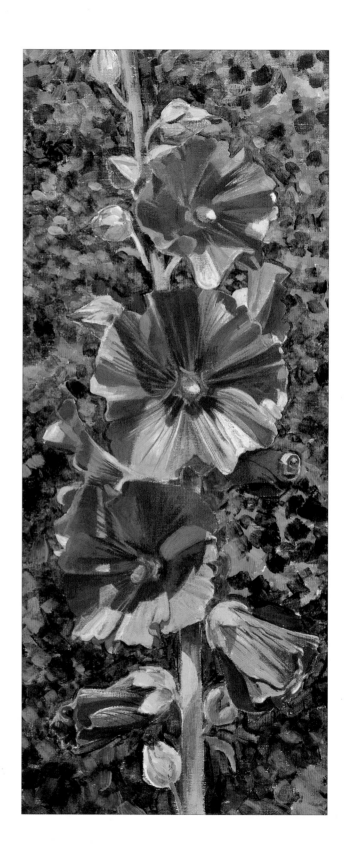

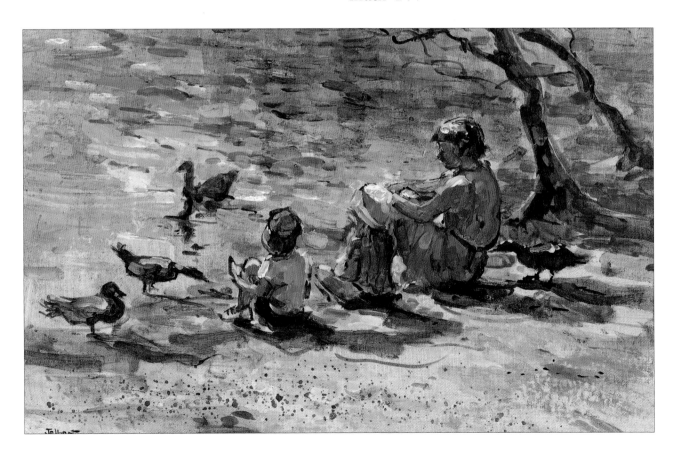

Materials

When choosing paints, brushes and other materials, always buy the best you can afford. Artists' quality colours, for example, are much purer and stronger than lesser qualities and, over a period of time, they will prove more economical to use.

Paints

Acrylic paints are available in a large range of luscious colours, similar to that for watercolours and oils. They may be bought in tubes, pots or tubs. Buy the best quality you can afford. Acrylic paints cannot be reworked when they dry out, so replace caps and lids immediately after use.

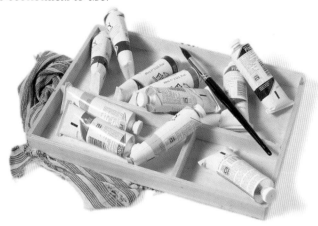

Brushes

The range of brushes available for acrylics is vast, and selecting the right ones to use can be quite daunting. They come in many different shapes and sizes and vary in quality. To start with, it is best to buy just one or two and then gradually build up a collection – again, buy the best you can afford. The artists who have written the various sections of this book have some useful advice. Wendy Jelbert suggests the following as a good general selection of brushes: flat brushes (Nos. 8, 12 and 18), round brushes (Nos. 3, 4, 6 and 8) and two rigger brushes (Nos. 0 and 1).

Landscape artist, David Hyde, recommends the following:

Hog bristle short flats – numbers 4 to 10 (up to no.12 if you paint larger than 30 x 40cm (12 x 16in). Keep your old, worn ones for adding texture.

Acrylic synthetic flats – in similar sizes for smoother, less textured paint application.

Acrylic synthetic rounds – numbers 1, 3 and 5 for detail.

Acrylic synthetic riggers – numbers 0 or 1 for fine lines, branches, twigs, etc.

Bristle or texturing fan brush – medium size for suggesting foreground foliage detail.

Carole Massey also uses a no. 8 filbert brush in one of the flower paintings demonstrated in this book.

Brushes must always be kept very clean. At the end of a painting session wash them out in a strong soapy solution.

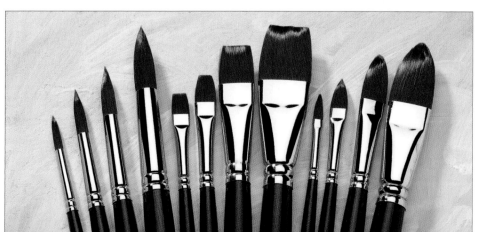

Papers and boards

Acrylics can be painted on to different types of paper and also on to many other, non-oily surfaces such as cardboard, canvas, wood and metal. You can use sheets of watercolour paper or pads of purpose-made acrylic papers.

Watercolour papers are available with different surface finishes: Hot Pressed (HP) is smooth; NOT/Cold Pressed is slightly textured; and Rough is heavily textured. All these papers are made in a range of weights (thicknesses), from 190gsm (90lb) to 640gsm (300lb).

Acrylic papers and boards usually have a canvas-like finish, which gives good 'character' to the surface. You can buy pads of acrylic papers. These are excellent value, as they support the work and offer a range of surfaces to choose from – canvas, NOT and Rough.

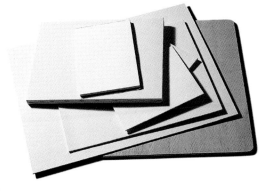

Stretching paper

If you are using the less heavy papers, you may need to stretch them to prevent cockling. Stretched paper always dries completely flat. You will need a sponge, a drawing board and four lengths of brown gum strip cut slightly longer than the sides of the paper. Wipe the wetted sponge over the drawing board, then place the paper on the board and wet that too. Stick down the gum strip, overlapping the paper by at least 6mm (¼in). Allow to dry naturally. When the finished painting is completely dry, remove it by cutting between the paper and gum strip using a craft knife.

Drawing board

A drawing board is useful for supporting individual sheets of paper. A 6mm (¼in) thick sheet of smooth plywood or MDF will prove ideal. Cut the board to suit your largest sheet of paper.

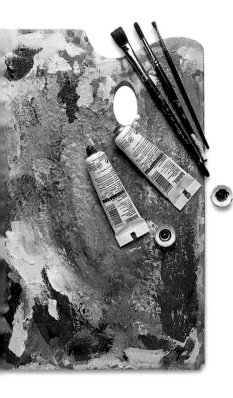

Palettes

Old china dinner plates make the best, and cheapest general purpose palettes when painting indoors. Make sure they have a shiny glazed surface so that they are easy to clean. Even dried paint will clean off easily after a short soak in warm water. Pick plates with little or no pattern and it is best if they are white or a neutral colour.

Acrylic stay-wet palettes can be used indoors and out (as long as the sun is not too hot). The stay-wet palette consists of a shallow tray with a tightfitting lid. It contains an absorbent layer (blotting paper or sponge) for you to soak in water. This is covered by a non-absorbent paper. Your colours are set out and mixed on this. As long as the lid is on, the colours within will remain usable for many days.

Traditional wooden palettes are useful when working outdoors on hot sunny days. Acrylic sticks permanently to wood so simply squeeze fresh paint on top as the sun dries it out. You can work quickly and, best of all, you never need clean your palette!

Tear-off palettes are useful when working outdoors on cooler days. They do not need cleaning so you do not need to carry extra water.

Mediums

In order to understand why and when a medium is to be used, we need to know a little about the 'make-up' of acrylic paint. All paint consists of a dry, coloured pigment held together with a liquid binder. In oil paint, this binder is a slow-drying linseed oil; in watercolour it is a soluble gum arabic; whereas in acrylic, it is a fast-drying synthetic resin. There is another component to the mix which is simply water. As acrylic paint dries, the water evaporates and the polymers in the resin bind together to make a permanent, flexible film. Water helps the paint flow and you can increase the flow by adding more water. However, if you add a lot of water, not only will the colour lose its brilliance, but over-dilution will prevent the polymers binding effectively and may cause an unstable layer in your work. The solution to producing transparent washes, or glazes, of acrylic colour is to dilute the paint with a medium – a synthetic resin with no pigment. Although it dries transparently, it is milky when you mix it with your paint. Normal amounts of water can be used to adjust the flow of the mix.

Mediums are available in a gloss or matt finish and as a gel or a more fluid consistency.

A retarder is a medium designed to slow down the drying time of acrylic paints, which some artists find useful if they want to use acrylic paints like oil paints and need plenty of time to blend and create softness.

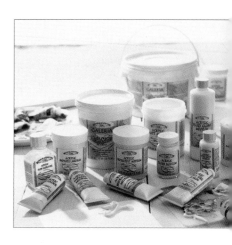

Materials for creating texture

Additives, in the form of **texture gels and pastes**, are great fun to use and offer the opportunity for creating some wonderful effects. These include such ingredients as glass beads, fibres, sand and grit. There is quite a wide range available, so talk to your local art shop about their characteristics before buying them.

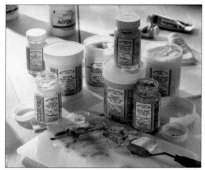

You can use other, less expensive materials to great effect. For example, **PVA glue** creates good watery textures, and **broken eggshells** make realistic rocks.

You can use **plastic food wrap** to conjure up beguiling abstract shapes for backgrounds, foregrounds, seascapes, flowers and woods. Working with this material needs practice, but the results are quite extraordinary and could solve a textural problem.

Different types of **salt** can be used with acrylics to create interesting textures. When salt is applied to watery acrylics, a unique series of star-like patterns and mottled markings are formed. You can use salt to create clouds, foam on rocks, snow flurries and massed foliage.

A **sponge** is good for both applying and lifting out colour.

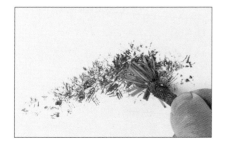

The **bungee brush** was invented by landscape painter, David Hyde, for creating texture and it can be made by modifying a bungee luggage strap. Simply cut off a length about 7.5cm (3in) long. Cut away some of the fabric sheath and smear it with epoxy adhesive to prevent fraying. Pull apart the individual strands of rubber and trim to the length required.

Other items

Pencil You can use a 6B graphite pencil for general sketching, and aquarelle pencils (which are also very soft) for quick colour notes. A 2B pencil is good for drawing a scene ready for painting.

Charcoal This can be used to draw out a scene on a primed board.

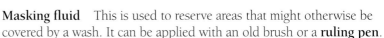

Putty eraser This very soft eraser is ideal for removing initial pencil lines without marking the surface of the paper.

Easel A lightweight, folding easel can be used in the studio or outside.

Masking fluid This is used to reserve areas that might otherwise be covered by a wash. It can be applied with an old brush or a **ruling pen**.

Masking tape Use this to secure paper to the drawing board. You could also use clips.

Absorbent paper Use this to lift out colour from washes and to clean brushes. It can also be used dampened to keep acrylic paints wet on the palette.

Water pots Use one pot to hold clean water for washes and another for rinsing out brushes.

Palette knife These come in a variety of shapes and sizes, and are used to apply acrylics as oils.

Rubber-tipped colour shaper This can be used to lift out colour and create texture.

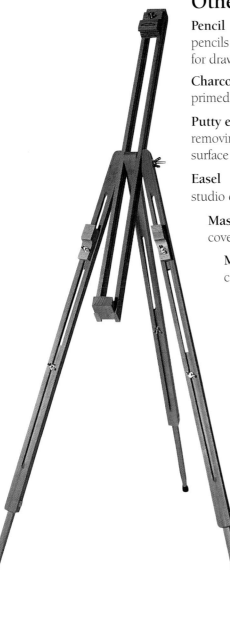

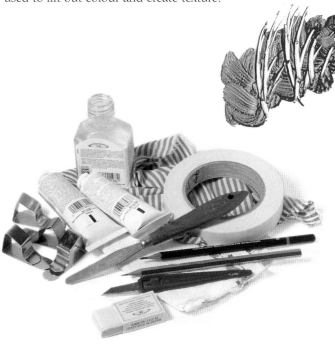

PAINTING WITH ACRYLICS

by Wendy Jelbert

Synthetic binders were discovered as painting mediums during the 1920s. Mexican muralists decided they needed an alternative to fresco and oil painting – they wanted a quick-drying paint which was unaffected by climatic changes. An ideal agent, which was already being used for moulded-plastic items, was discovered and when this was added to the paint it created all the qualities that the artists were seeking – a paint with fast-drying qualities, and with a freshness and permanence that made it suitable for murals and public buildings. Actual acrylic paints were first used in America in the 1950s by colour field artists such as Morris Louis.

Acrylics are amazingly versatile. Watercolour and oil techniques can be used with this remarkable medium, as well as pure acrylic techniques which are exciting and open up all sorts of creative possibilities – you can even mix all the techniques together in one painting. With practice, a vibrancy and spontaneity can be achieved that will inspire you to experiment even further.

Other advantages are that acrylics can be used on a wide range of surfaces – canvas, paper, wood, metal and plaster – and their fast-drying qualities allow colours to be applied quickly without disturbing the layers beneath.

I have taught painting in all media for twenty-five years and acrylics have not always been popular with my students. They have complained about the fast-drying qualities and the brightness of the colours. Slow workers have not always been able to achieve the effects they wanted. However, there are now special palettes available which keep the paints moist, and you can add acrylic mediums to the paints, which retard the drying time so that you can blend and manipulate the colours as you work.

In this section my aim is to demonstrate the versatility and exciting qualities of acrylics, showing how they are a medium of comparative freedom and not one of limitations. Step-by-step demonstrations guide you through all the techniques, and a series of paintings illustrate the points I make. So, if you are a beginner – or if you are rediscovering acrylics for a second time – I hope you will find inspiration in the following pages and that you will soon be painting pictures you are proud of.

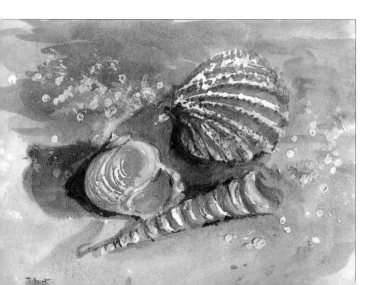

Shells
20.5 x 15.5cm (8 x 6in)
These shells had lots of surface texture, and I used the exciting impasto technique (see page 18) to recreate this on the paper.

Opposite
Sea Shore
18 x 24.5cm (7 x 9¾in)

This simple seascape shows how effective a striking contrast of colour can be. Here, the blues (painted as simple graded washes in the sea areas) work well against the tones of yellow ochre and burnt sienna.

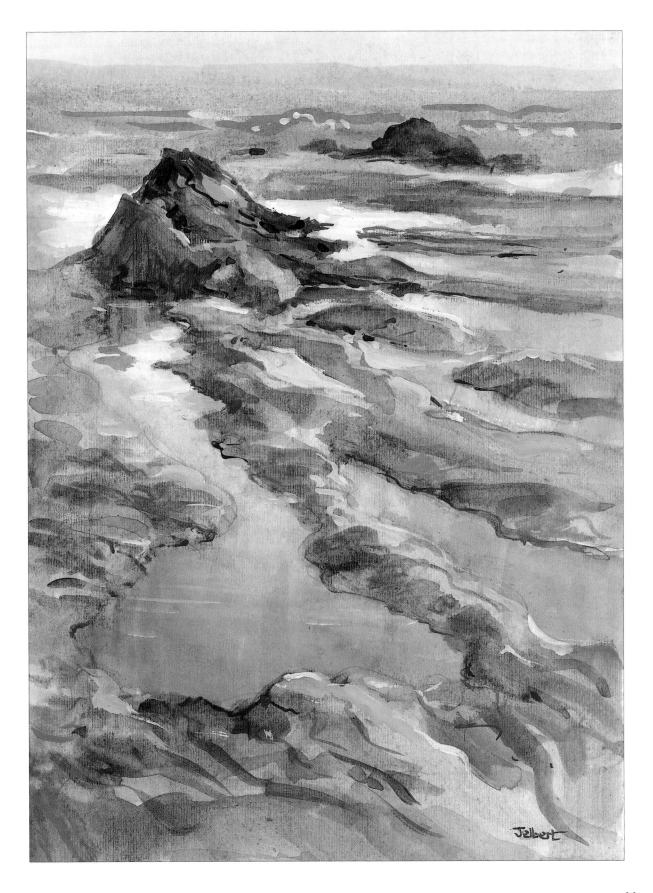

My palette

Below is my stay-wet palette with some of my favourite colours. These include: lemon yellow, azo yellow medium, napthol red light, permanent alizarin crimson, ultramarine blue, phthalo blue (red shade), cerulean blue, olive green, phthalo green (blue shade), yellow ochre, raw umber, titanium white, burnt sienna, dioxazine purple, benzimidazolone maroon.

In the projects in this section I have added Payne's gray, cadmium orange, permanent sap green, olive green, fluorescent pink and cadmium red light to this basic palette.

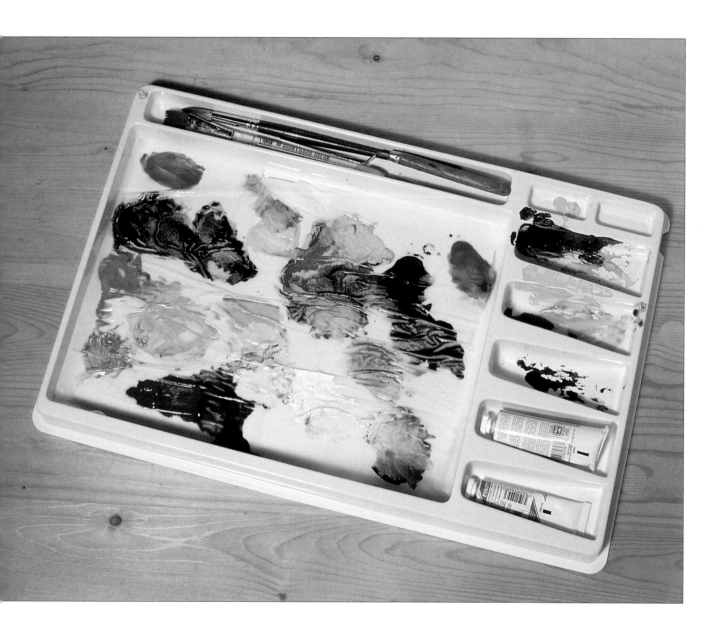

My sketchbook

My sketchbook goes with me everywhere and I use it to capture the atmosphere of scenes *in situ*. I plan out future paintings with several preliminary working sketches. I find it fun to experiment with various alternatives – ink or pencil sketches, quick colourful tryouts and variations-on-a-theme. Planning and sketching in this way is most important, as it can avoid mistakes that might otherwise occur back in the studio.

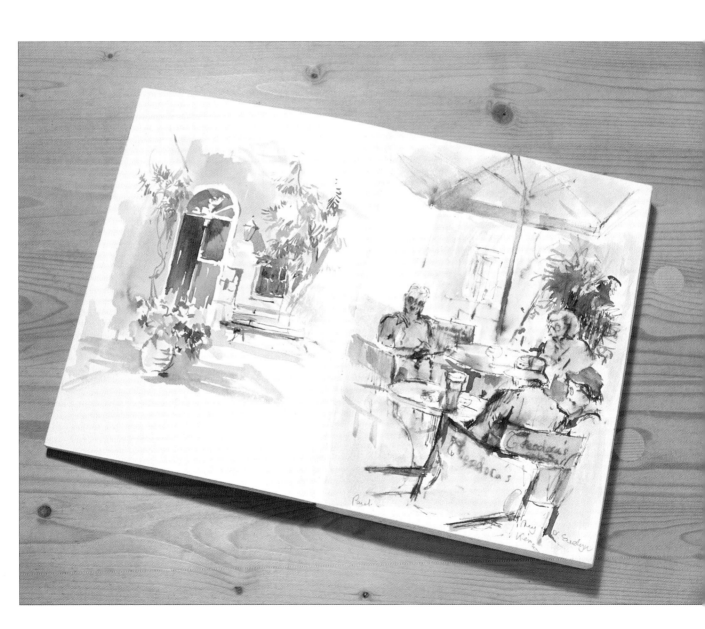

Colour mixing

Colour mixing is one of the most important skills of a competent artist.
Acrylic paints can be mixed with each other to create different colours,
mixed with white to make paler tints, or diluted with water to create subtle,
translucent tones. Learning how acrylics behave when diluted or mixed
with each other takes a lot of practice, much like a piano student learning
scales. There are no short cuts – you must carefully work up your skill in
order to succeed. You could buy every available colour but, apart from
the expense, you would still not be able to create the subtle tones that
colour mixing can achieve. Here are some of the colour mixes I use for the
paintings in this section.

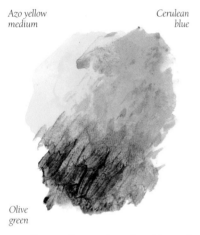

Azo yellow medium

Cerulean blue

Olive green

Azo yellow medium and cerulean blue make
good 'safe' greens for foliage and trees. Mix
them with a ready-made olive green to vary
tonal values.

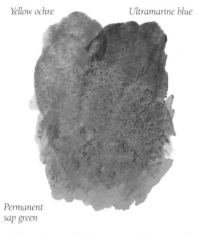

Yellow ochre

Ultramarine blue

Permanent sap green

Yellow ochre and ultramarine blue provide
other tones of green. Introduce ready-made
sap green to create even richer colours.

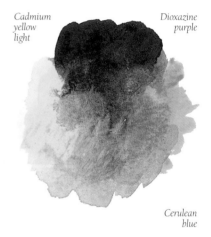

Cadmium yellow light

Dioxazine purple

Cerulean blue

Adding purple to the yellow and blue mix
makes a darker green. More yellow makes
it a sunny green, and more blue creates a
shaded tone.

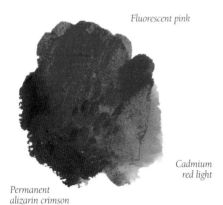

Fluorescent pink

Cadmium red light

Permanent alizarin crimson

Mixes of these colours are ideal for bright
vibrant flowers such as geraniums. Use
more crimson to give deeper, darker tones.
Add more water or pink to create lighter,
brighter effects.

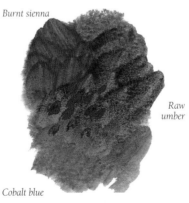

Burnt sienna

Raw umber

Cobalt blue

These three colours make shades that are
ideal for rocks or tree bark. Use more
burnt sienna for warm, light areas, and
more raw umber and cobalt blue for deep,
dark shadows.

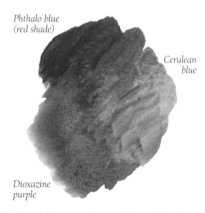

Phthalo blue (red shade)

Cerulean blue

Dioxazine purple

Skies and seas require a wide variety of
colours and tones. This combination of
colours will help to create a lot of them
– use all three together for rich deep tones
and mix them with titanium white for
lighter tints.

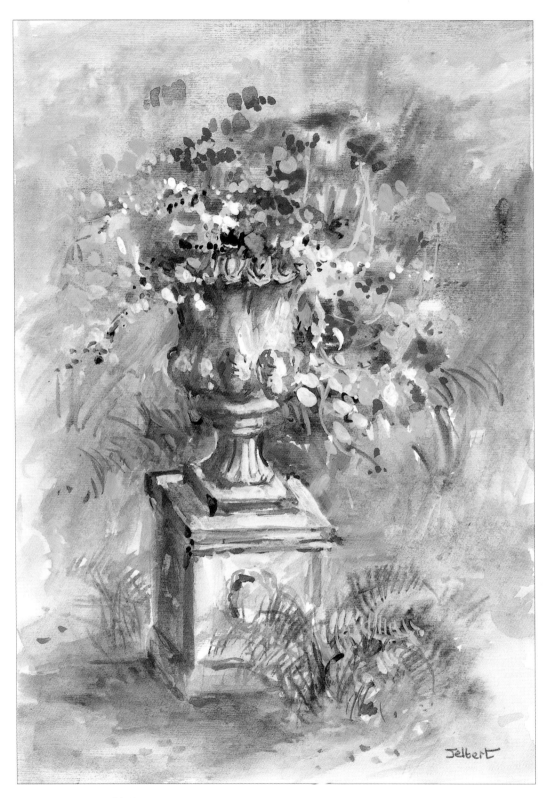

Geraniums in an Old Urn
17.5 x 25.5cm (6¾ x 10in)
This painting includes many of the colour combinations shown opposite.

Playing with acrylics

Painting with acrylics can be great fun as this medium is so versatile. You can use the colours in the same way as either watercolours or oils – so it offers many exciting challenges to the beginner and to the experienced artist.

Watercolour techniques

When used as watercolours, acrylics can be gentle and watery, bold and vibrant or wet into wet – in fact some of the so-called watercolour exhibitions in London comprise 75% acrylic paintings!

Acrylics also have the advantage that, when dry, the washes are so permanent that glazes can be added without the fear of disturbing the undercolours. If you need to change the colours, you can wash them off immediately, before drying, and start all over again without any change beneath.

Here are just a few of the water-colour techniques that can be worked with acrylics. The list is by no means complete and I am sure that, with a little experience, you will soon discover how to create many other different effects.

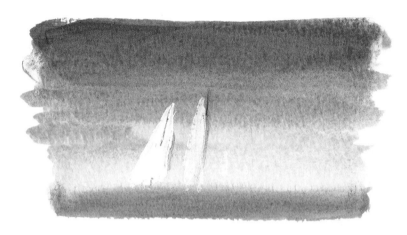

Simple graded wash

A graded wash is very suitable for a simple sky. Add water to blue acrylic to form a wash and then, using a large brush, lay a band of colour across the top of the paper. Add more water to the wash and lay another band of this tone slightly overlapping the first one. Continue adding more water and laying in more dilute colour to form a graded wash from dark to light. In this example, I stopped the wash on the horizon line and then laid in a band of strong colour for the sea. The sails were painted with neat titanium white.

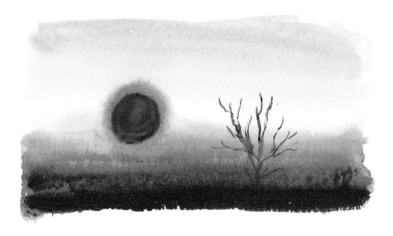

Blended washes

Blending two simple graded washes together can create some interesting effects. Lay in a simple graded wash in one colour, working from the top of the paper to the mid point. Turn the paper round and lay a contrasting wash down to the mid point, allowing the weakest tone of this colour to blend with the first wash. In this study of blended washes, the outer edge of the sun was painted while the washes were still damp. The paint was allowed to dry then the sun and tree were painted in.

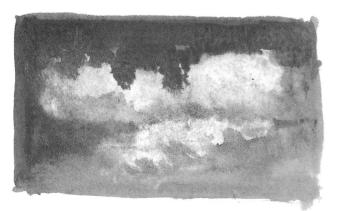

Lifting out

This technique can be used to create pale, soft-edged images such as clouds. Lay a wash on wetted paper and then press absorbent paper on to the wet paint to lift out some of the colour and create a lighter image in the paint. In this sky study I introduced greys into the bottom of the lifted-out clouds to create a more realistic effect.

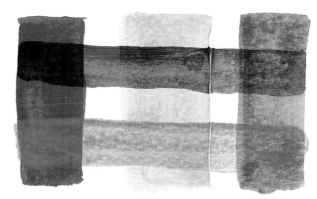

Glazes

Diluted acrylics are transparent and can be glazed over other dry colours to good effect. Experiment with bands of colour at right-angles to each other. Blue glazes are good for shadows, yellow ones for sunny studies.

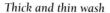

Wet into wet

This flower study of poppies started with a fusion of colours created by the wet-into-wet technique. Wet the paper with clean water and then drop diluted colours on to the wet surface. Tilt the paper from side to side and top to bottom, allowing the colours to blend together. This is a fascinating technique and with a little practice you will soon learn how to control paint flow.

Thick and thin wash

If you partly dilute the paint with water you create a wash containing blobs of neat colour, and this thick and thin mix can be used to create interesting effects. Dip a brush into the mix and skim it over the dry or wetted surface of the paper to create patches of deep colour on a wash of the same colour. In this tree study I first laid a blue wash over the paper and, while this was still damp, I painted the trees using the a thick and thin mix of brown.

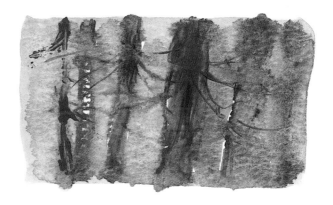

Oil techniques

Acrylics may be used straight from the tube, using a palette knife or a brush, in a similar way to oil paints. Here are a few techniques for you to experiment with. Special mediums may be mixed with acrylic colours to retard the drying time and improve the flow. There are many mediums to choose from, so consult with your local art supplier.

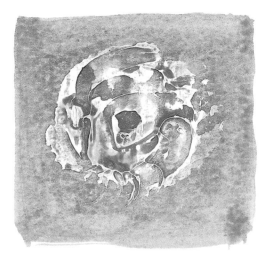

Impasto

Impasto is the application of thick layers of paint straight from the tube using a brush or palette knife to create lovely textures. You can also mix paint with acrylic impasto medium to create much heavier patterning. Whichever method you use, the textures can be left as they are or, when they are completely dry, you can apply a glaze over parts of them. This is a lovely way to create designs on pots, or to reproduce the texture of old stone walls or steps.

Scumbling

Paint one colour on to a dry surface. When this is dry, use a brush or palette knife to drag another, quite stiff colour on top, letting the first colour 'gleam' through in places. This technique is useful for suggesting snow or rocks in a mountain scene.

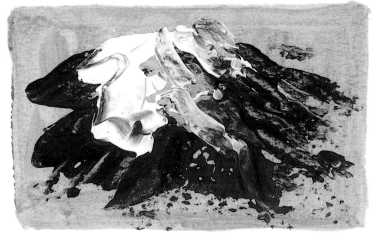

Painting with a palette knife

Try painting a picture using just a palette knife and paint straight from the tube. Experiment with different blade shapes and adventurous strokes! These juicy, textured effects are ideal for architectural subjects but they can also be used for lots of other subjects. For example, here is a log fire with flames and smoke, painted entirely with a palette knife.

Other techniques

Here are two other techniques for you to experiment with. Masking fluid creates controlled highlights, and can be combined with any of the painting techniques discussed on the previous pages. The random lifting out technique, which can only be worked with acrylic paint, creates an exciting and free start to a painting.

These 'tricks-of-the-trade' are fun to play with, they will enhance your work and they offer you a variety of ways to paint many different subjects. Hopefully, they will fire up your imagination to paint even more diverse subject matter.

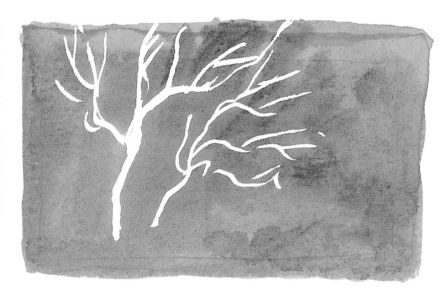

Using masking fluid

Masking fluid repels paint so it can be used to retain areas of white paper. Alternatively, it can be applied on to dry painted areas that are to be overpainted with, say, a glaze. Apply the masking fluid with a drawing pen or an old brush and allow it to dry. Paint over it and then, when all the paint is dry, rub off the masking fluid to expose the white paper or undercolour. Do not apply too heavy a layer of paint on the masking fluid, as this may make it difficult to remove. Use masking fluid for images such as the trees shown here, or for small details of plants or architectural features.

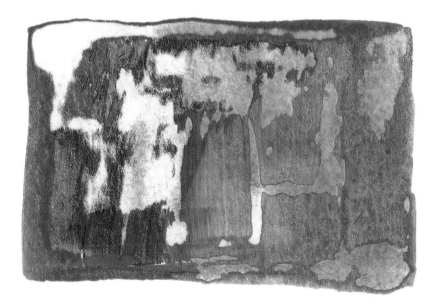

Random lifting out

This technique relies on the fact that although acrylic paint is diluted with water, it becomes waterproof when dry. This characteristic can be used to create some exciting, uncontrolled results. Apply different thicknesses of paint to the paper, partly dry the surface (with a hairdryer), then submerge the paper in a bowl of clean water and rub the painted surface with your fingers. Some of the still-wet colour will lift off and leave plain paper (or muted colours) in random patterns.

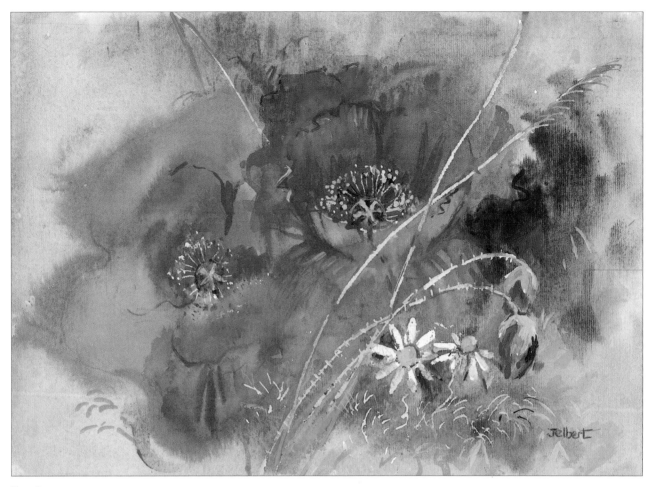

Poppies
25.5 x 18.0cm (10 x 7in)

Poppies are one of the most popular subjects to paint. They are so perfect for watercolour techniques, as they ebb and flow into each other and the surrounding areas.

I sketched in the poppy heads, daisies, buds and stalks with a pencil, then applied coloured masking fluid with a drawing pen.

When the masking fluid was dry, I wetted the paper and painted around the flower heads using a light green mixture of yellow ochre and olive green. While this was still wet, I quickly painted in the flowers using tones of red and pink, letting the colours mix on the paper. I added dark accents with blues and greens to the right of the poppies and seed heads. When the paint was thoroughly dry, I carefully rubbed off the masking fluid.

I intensified the darks in the background, detailed the seed heads with yellow ochre and olive green and painted in the buds and daisies with a rigger. Finally, I washed over some of the white daisy petals with pale blue tones, and allowed others to remain light.

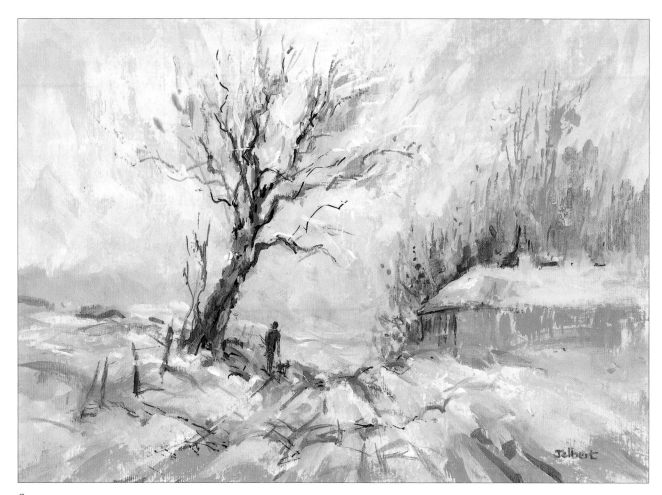

Snow scene

25.5 x 18cm (10 x 7in)

This simple landscape composition is painted quite loosely, using relatively dry mixes of acrylic paint as oils.

I used a rigger brush and raw umber to sketch in the tree, path and house. When these marks had dried, I covered the whole surface with a watery covering of yellow ochre as an undercoat to unite all the elements of the painting.

I applied a mix of cobalt blue and titanium white to the sky and distant trees, and used a slightly lighter mix for the roof. I used dioxazine purple and titanium white in the foreground and in the shadowed areas under the tree and across the path.

The sky, distant trees and foreground areas were completed using thick layers of blues and purples, allowing small chinks of the original yellow ochre to show through and add sparkle. I painted in the house, pulling colour into the surrounding area of snow and across the path to the tree. I then used the palette knife to thicken the snow with small dabs of lighter blues.

Details of the tree and fence posts were added using a rigger brush with burnt sienna and blues. Finally, I painted in the figure and dog as a focal point.

Painting skies

Skies can be magical, and I love to just sit and watch the ever-changing shapes and colours. Even a cloudless blue sky will change through the course of the day. For a landscape to be successful, the sky should be painted in sympathy with the surroundings below – choose a simple sky if the main subject is full of detail. On these pages I show you three skies, each painted using a different technique.

Simple sky – graded wash

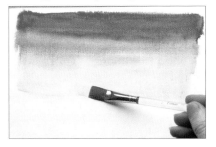

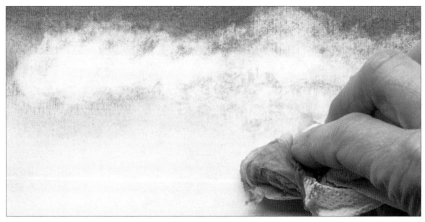

1. Dampen the paper with clean water. Then, working with long horizontal strokes of a large flat brush, lay in a graded wash of ultramarine blue. Work down the paper, laying in more dilute tones towards the horizon.

2. Dampen a piece of absorbent paper and gently dab out some clouds. Work quickly, using a clean part of the paper each time you lift out the colour.

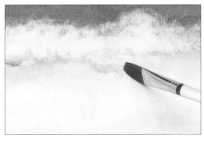

3. Mix a fluid grey wash from ultramarine blue and a touch of burnt sienna, and then paint shadowed areas into the undersides of the clouds.

4. Dilute the grey mix slightly, then paint in the edges of the more distant clouds to complete the sky.

Sunset – wet into wet

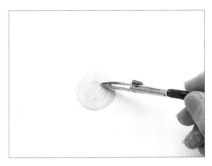

1. Use masking fluid and a drawing pen to create a rough circular shape for the sun. Leave to dry.

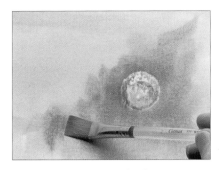

2. Wet the paper with clean water. Mix azo yellow medium with cadmium red light and lay an orange wash across the paper. Add a touch of fluorescent pink to the mix and wash this around the sun, allowing the edges to blend with the still-damp yellow.

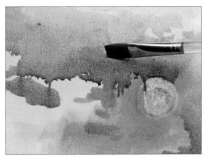

3. Use a wash of dioxazine purple to lay in some clouds around the sun. Add touches of ultramarine blue, dioxazine purple and clean water to the clouds to create shape and form.

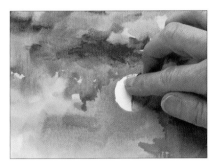

4. When all the paint is dry, rub off the masking fluid to reveal white paper.

5. Now use diluted azo yellow medium to paint the sun, weakening the colour as you work across the shape. Use dioxazine purple to lay a few wisps of cloud across the sun.

Stormy sky – oil technique

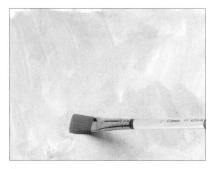

1. Using various strengths of colour, 'flick' yellow ochre in all directions over the paper. Leave to dry.

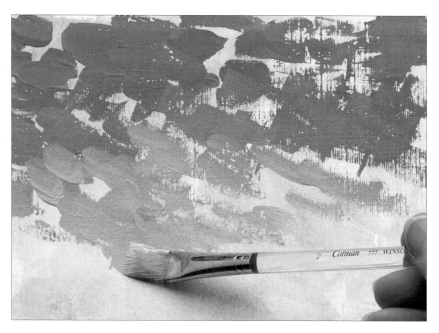

2. Mix a mid blue from ultramarine blue and titanium white. Dab this colour over the yellow, leaving some of the yellow to peep through. Add more white to the blue mix as you work down the paper, and gradually introduce softer strokes of the brush.

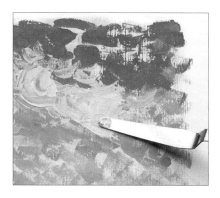

3. Add touches of burnt sienna and ultramarine blue to titanium white, then use a palette knife to lay in some clouds; use the blade to create swirls and texture.

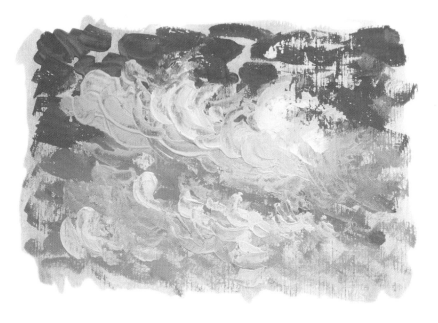

4. Finally, add highlights in the clouds using titanium white with a hint of burnt sienna.

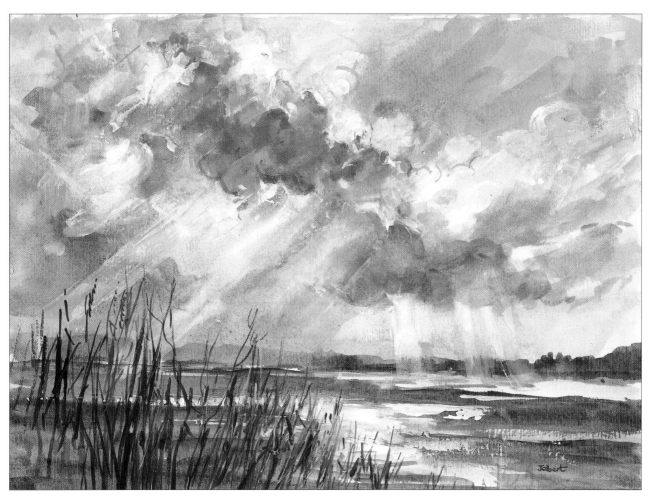

Stormy Clouds
34 x 24.5cm (13½ x 9¾in)

This dramatic sky painting captures the feel of a stormy yet sunny day. The sun rays bursting through gaps in the menacing clouds highlight the middle distance. This light area provides a stark contrast between the dark background and the silhouetted detail of the foreground foliage.

Sunlit Window

I came across this colourful wall whilst on a painting holiday in Brittany with some of my students. I made a pencil sketch composition, and I also took a few photographs to remind me of the colours and textures. The impasto technique is excellent for depicting the texture of the rough stone wall and, for this demonstration, I also use glazing and scumbling to reproduce the colours of the stonework. Masking fluid helps accentuate the highlights, whilst the wet-into-wet technique is perfect for depicting the riotous colours of the geraniums. I painted this picture on a 405 x 305mm (16 x 12in) sheet of 300gsm (140lb) paper.

You will need

Titanium white
Burnt sienna
Raw umber
Payne's gray
Dioxazine purple
Cadmium orange
Azo yellow medium
Permanent sap green
Olive green
Fluorescent pink
Ultramarine blue
Yellow ochre
2B pencil
Masking fluid and a drawing pen
Palette knife
No. 10 flat brush
No. 6 round brush

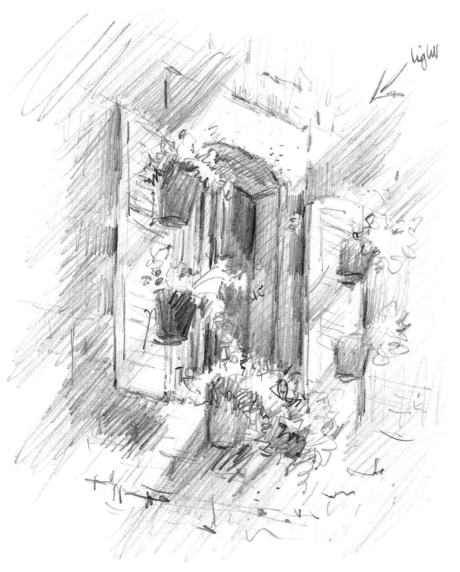

Pencil sketch drawn on location. Compare this 'squared-up' composition with the distorted image of the photographic reference.

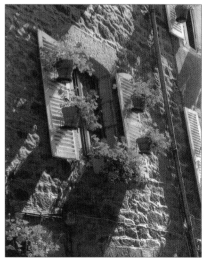

Photographs are useful as reminders of colour and texture. However, they often show lots of extraneous detail and can have peculiar perspectives. This one, for example, was taken in a narrow lane and I could not move back far enough to get the uprights vertical.

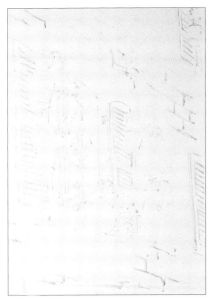

1. Use a 2B pencil to lightly draw in the main elements of the composition. Then, using masking fluid (mixed with a touch of colour) and a drawing pen, mask out some of the mortar and the louvres on the window shutters.

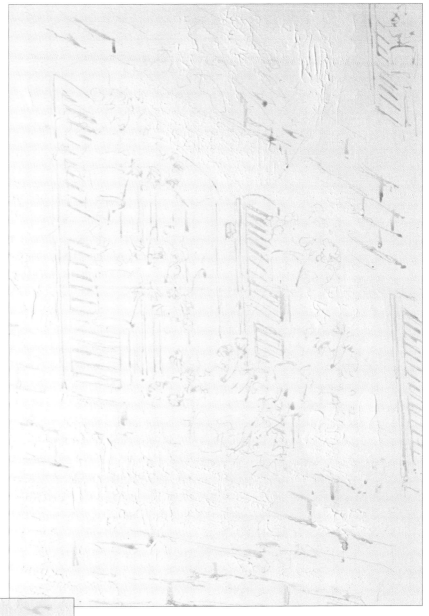

2. Use a palette knife and titanium white straight from the tube to apply paint to the stone wall. Work short horizontal and vertical strokes to create different textures. Leave to dry.

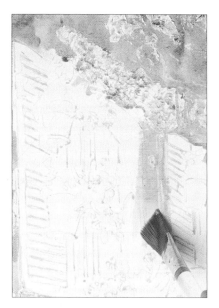

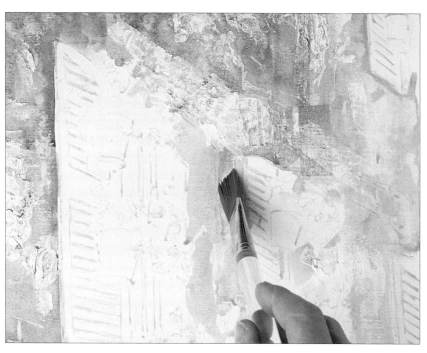

3. Use the flat brush to lay a wash of burnt sienna and raw umber over the stone walls. Leave to dry.

4. Mix Payne's gray with a little titanium white, then glaze over all the stonework (except the lintels) to vary the tone. Allow the colour to concentrate in the deep recesses of the impasto texture.

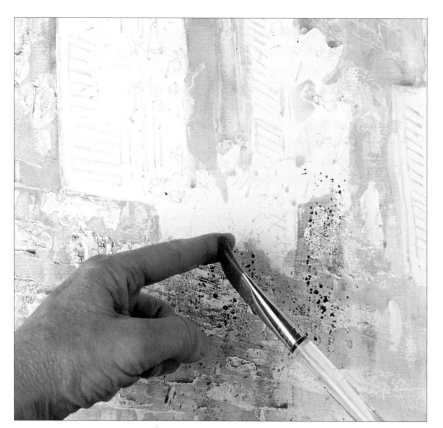

5. Mix a very wet wash of dioxazine purple and raw umber, then drag your finger across the brush to splatter the paint randomly over the painted stonework.

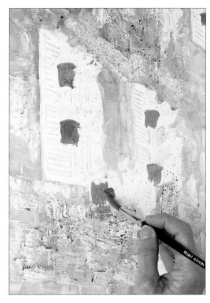

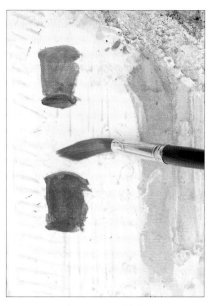

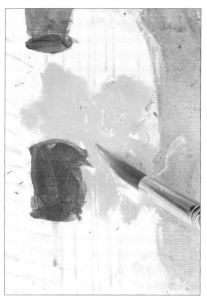

6. Mix burnt sienna with cadmium orange, then use the round brush to paint in the flower pots in various tones. Add touches of raw umber to create shadows and shape.

7. Re-wet the areas of foliage.

8. Paint azo yellow medium, wet into wet, into areas of foliage, then drop in some permanent sap green.

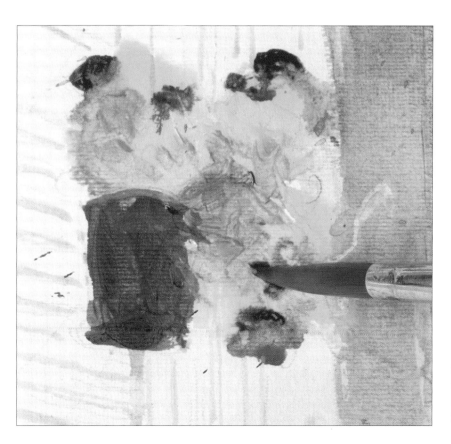

9. Add a few touches of olive green to the foliage to create shape, then drop in fluorescent pink for the flower heads.

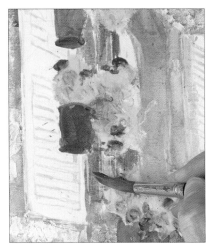

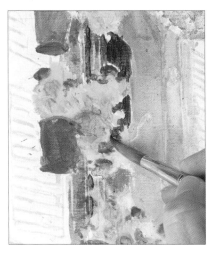

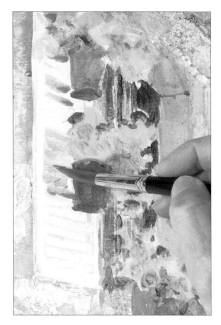

10. Block in the dark windows, using a mix of ultramarine blue, azo yellow medium and a touch of permanent sap green.

11. Use dioxazine purple to create deeper shadows in the windows and define the outline of the foliage.

12. Start to define the window shutters by painting the louvres with a mix of ultramarine blue and a touch of permanent sap green. Leave to dry.

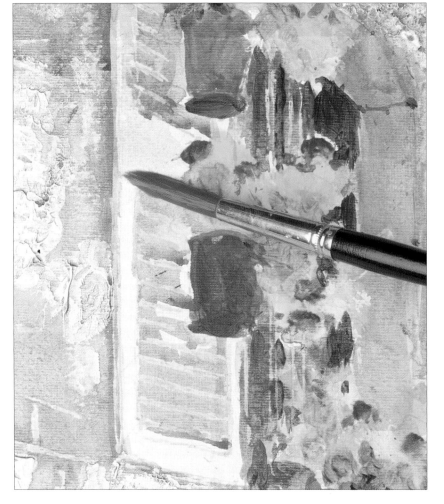

13. Now apply a weak yellow ochre glaze over the window shutters.

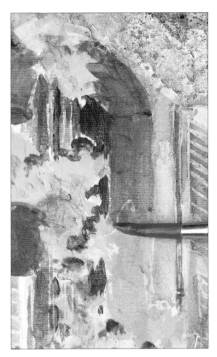

14. Add more colour to the window reveals using a mix of burnt sienna with a touch of yellow ochre. Vary the tone to create shape and shadows. Leave to dry.

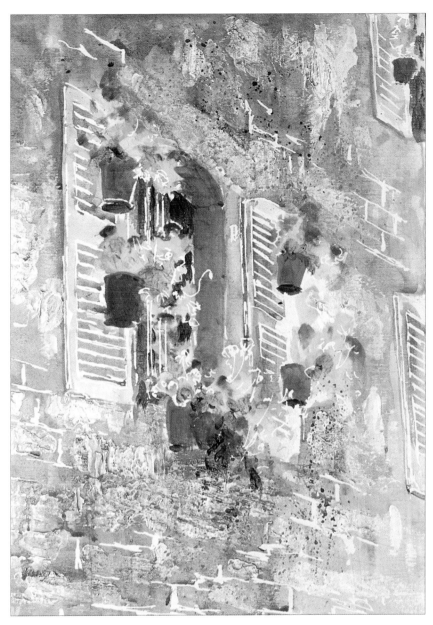

15. Carefully rub off all the masking fluid.

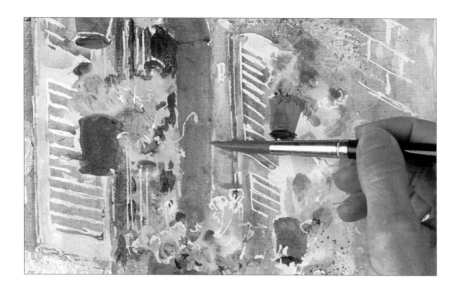

16. Glaze diluted washes of the background tones over the stonework, foliage and flowers to soften all the exposed areas of white paper.

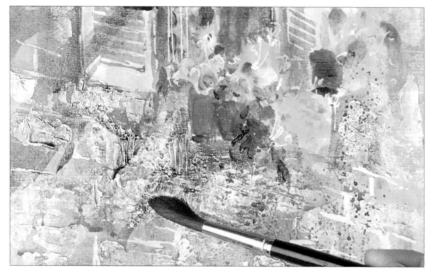

17. Mix dioxazine purple with ultramarine blue and a touch of burnt sienna, then add shadows across the walls, shutters, flower pots and foliage. Leave to dry.

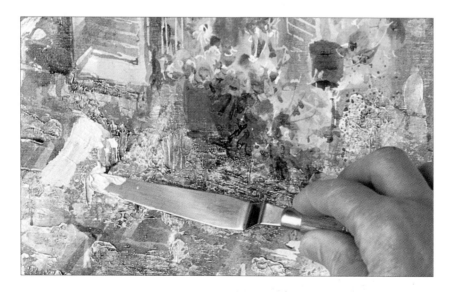

18. Finally, mix titanium white and yellow ochre straight from the tube, then use a palette knife to scumble a thin layer of colour over the sunlit areas of stonework.

Opposite
The finished painting.

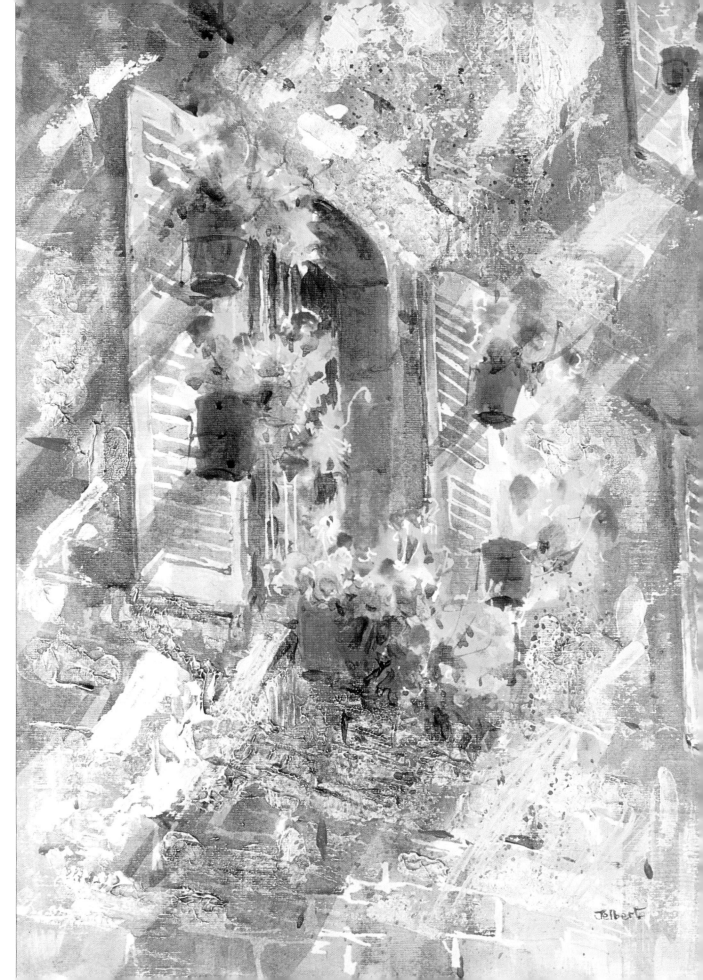

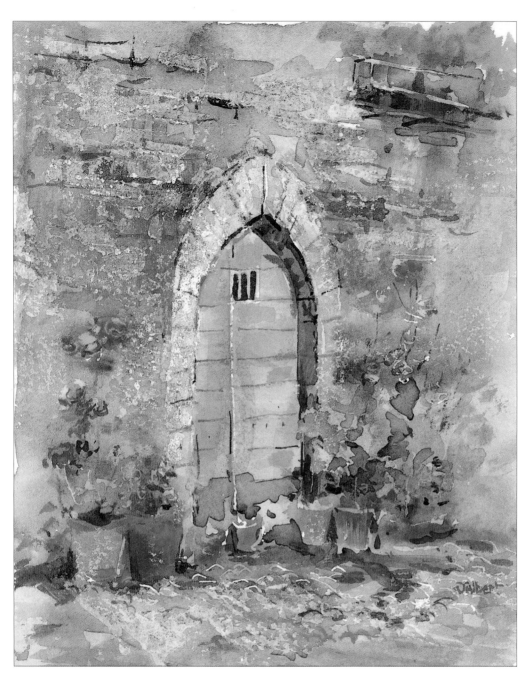

Tuscany Door with Flowers
15.5 x 18.5cm (6 x 7¼in)

I used the impasto texturing technique described on page 18 to produce the weathered appearance of these old walls. The light blue of the door contrasts well against the greys, burnt sienna and yellow ochre tones used for the stonework.

Opposite
Greek Doorway with Old Chair
37 x 49.5cm (14½ x 19½in)

The atmosphere of this painting is created by the contrast between the light and dark areas. I loved the sunlit vines, the reflected light on the old chair and the foreground thistles, all of which were painted with masking fluid at an early stage. I also used an assortment of different textures when painting the walls and foreground areas.

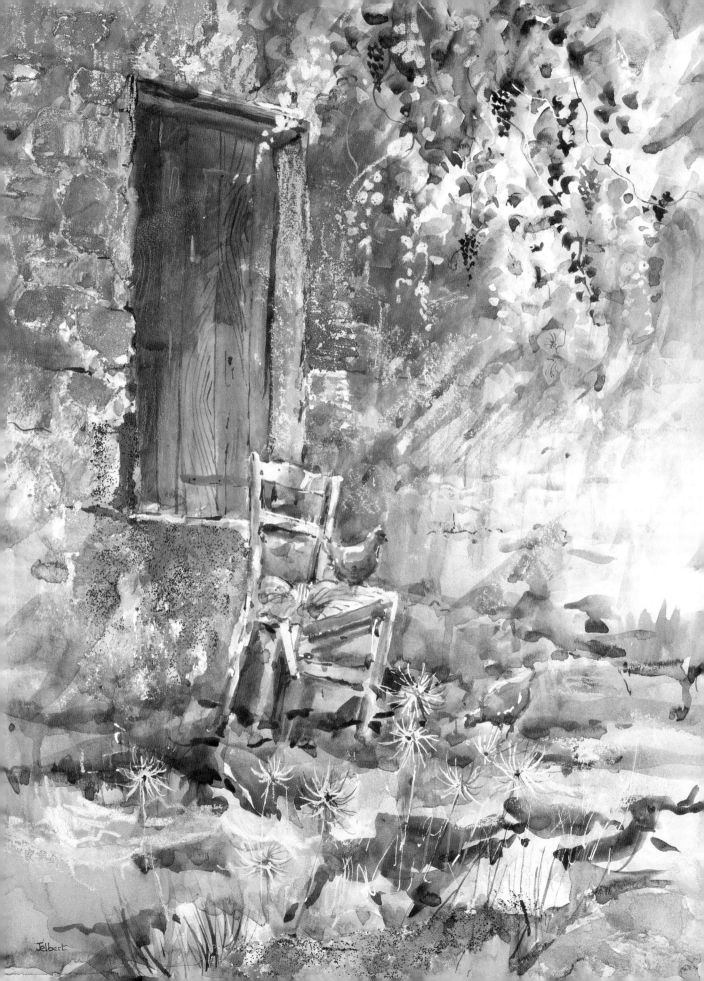

Farmyard

I love painting animals in general, and chickens in particular. I used two reference photographs to compose this painting – one of a roadside fence, the other of a group of chickens.

In this demonstration I use simple washes, controlled and random lifting out, impasto, thick and thin, glazing and scumbling techniques. The picture is painted on a 405 x 305mm (16 x 12in) sheet of 300gsm (140lb) watercolour paper.

You will need
Cerulean blue
Ultramarine blue
Permanent sap green
Olive green
Burnt sienna
Yellow ochre
Dioxazine purple
Azo yellow medium
Cadmium red light
Titanium white
Impasto medium
2B pencil
No. 10 Flat brush
No. 6 Round brush
No. 1 Rigger brush
Palette knives
Absorbent paper
Washing-up bowl
Masking tape

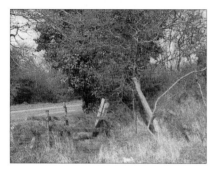
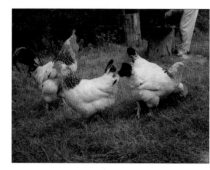

The two photographs used to compose the painting. When working from photographs, I usually sketch the outlines straight on to the painting paper. However, I have also included a pencil sketch to show you how I combined details from each photograph to form the final composition.

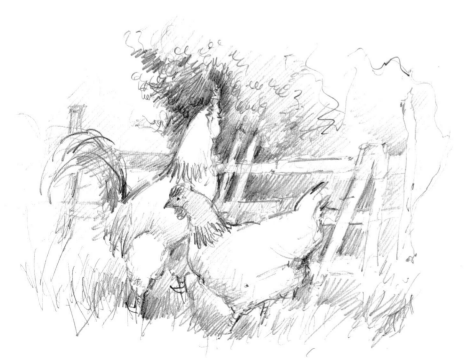

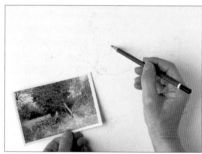

1. Use a 2B pencil to draw the outlines of the main elements on to your paper.

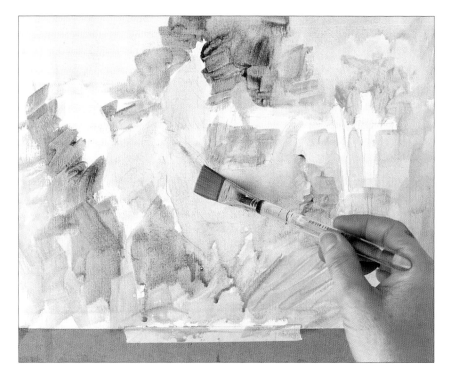

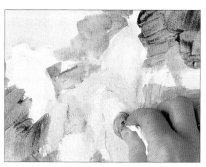

3. While the paint is still damp, lift out some colour from the hen using damp absorbent paper.

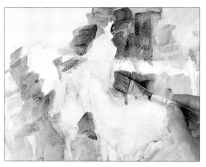

2. Use the flat brush to lay a pale wash of cerulean blue over the sky and chickens, then lay a pale wash of ultramarine blue mixed with permanent sap green over the foliage. Add more blue and some olive green to the mix, then block in the foliage around the cockerel. Use the thick and thin technique to brush ultramarine blue over both chickens.

4. Reinstate the dark areas using the flat brush with mixes of olive green and ultramarine blue.

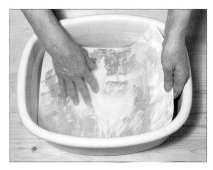

5. Allow the painting to partly dry, then immerse the paper in a bowl of clean water. Rub the surface of the painting gently, so that the image breaks up slightly.

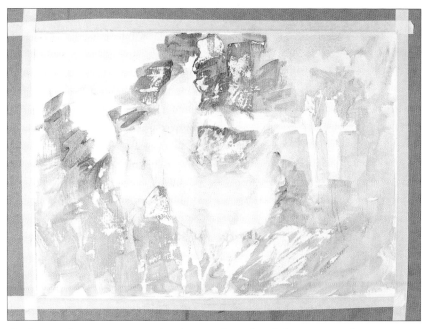

6. Secure the wet paper to the drawing board with long strips of masking tape, then allow the paper to dry on a flat surface.

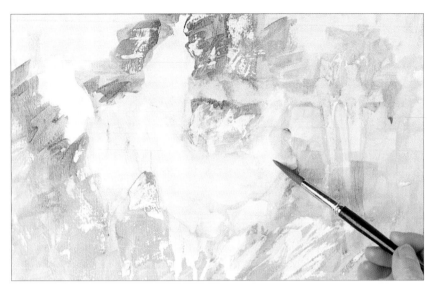

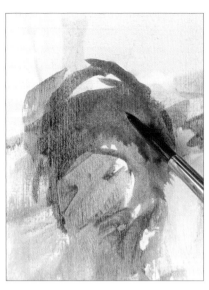

7. Mix yellow ochre, burnt sienna and a touch of ultramarine blue, then use the round brush to wash in the fence. Add touches of the same colour to the chickens to define form.

8. Paint in the cockerel's tail feathers using mixes of dioxazine purple and ultramarine blue.

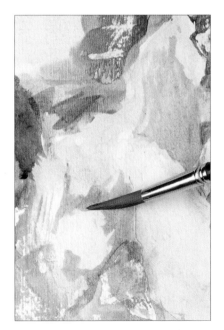

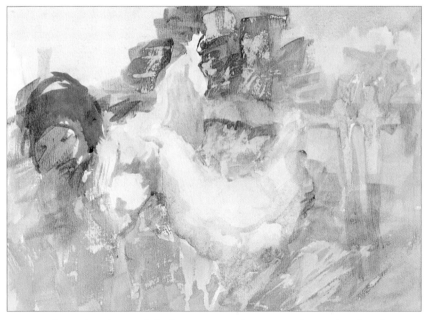

9. Dilute the mix and define the cockerel's neck feathers and legs.

10. Work up the shape of the hen in a similar way to the cockerel with a dilute wash of cerulean blue. Then, using azo yellow medium and the flat brush, glaze across the grass and foliage to colour any remaining white areas.

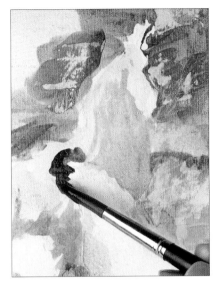

11. Mix cadmium red light, burnt sienna and a touch of dioxazine purple, then paint in the hen's comb and wattle.

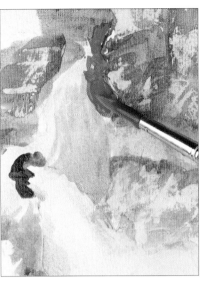

12. Mix cadmium red light with some azo yellow medium to make a brighter red, then paint in the cockerel's comb and wattle.

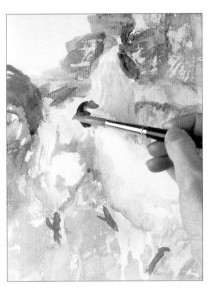

13. Paint the chickens' legs with the two red mixes, then add shadow and form to their heads. Paint the beaks with yellow ochre.

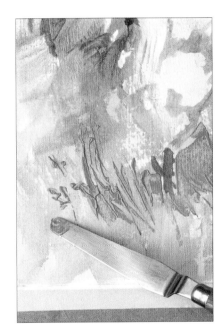

14. Work detail into the foreground grasses and foliage using a palette knife and a dry mix of permanent sap green with a touch of olive green.

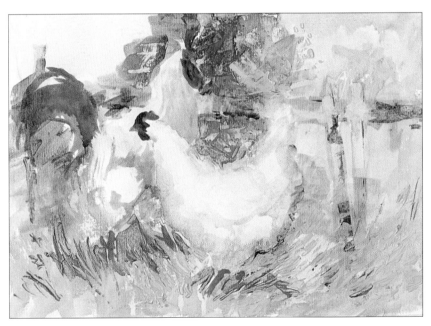

15. Add touches of cerulean blue and titanium white to the green mix, then continue to develop the grass using variations of tone and different strokes of the palette knife. Mix permanent sap green with dioxazine purple and burnt sienna, then scumble this colour over parts of the fence to create shadows and the appearance of age.

39

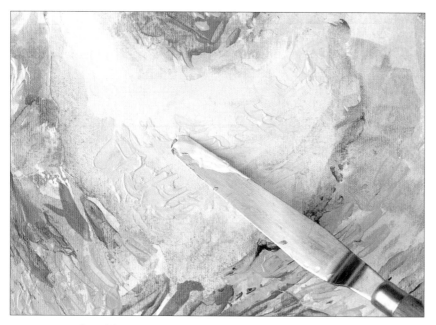

16. Mix cerulean blue, titanium white and impasto medium, then create feathers with a palette knife to 'fatten up' the chickens.

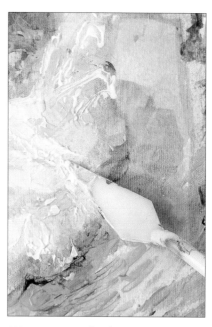

17. Mix a touch of impasto medium with titanium white, then add highlights on the feathers. Use a pointed palette knife to add fine detail.

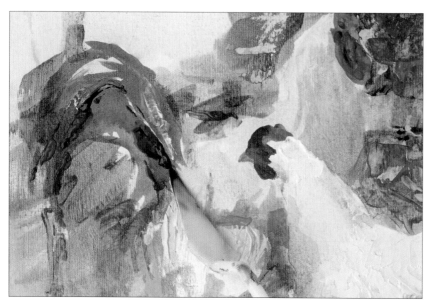

18. Add a touch of cerulean blue to the mix, then apply highlights to the cockerel's tail feathers. Now add dioxazine purple to the mix and define some darker feathers. Use the same mix to define a few dark areas on the bodies of both chickens.

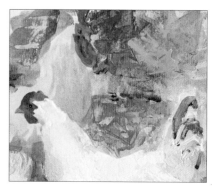

19. Use a palette knife and a mix of ultramarine blue and olive green to add definition to the hen's tail feathers. Use the same mix and the round brush to define the eyes of both birds.

20. Mix a grey from burnt sienna and cerulean blue, then use criss-cross strokes of a rigger brush to paint in the cockerel's neck feathers. Make a darker mix and add more brush strokes to define shape, and to create a dark area behind the hen's head. Mix burnt sienna with a touch of ultramarine blue, then work the hen's neck feathers in the same way.

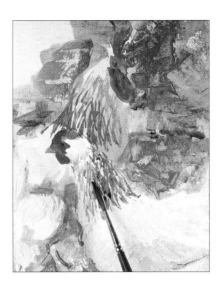

The finished painting.

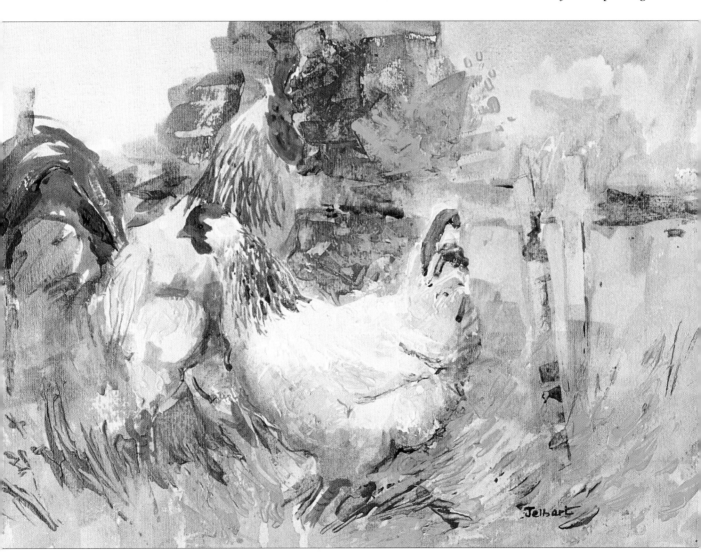

LANDSCAPES IN ACRYLICS

by David Hyde

"I can't get on with acrylics; they dry too quickly."
"I find acrylics too bright and the effects not very subtle." "I much prefer a more traditional style of painting." These are all sentiments I once shared. These 'problems' still cause people concern, and I hope that if you share these views, your heart and mind can be won over.

Acrylic is arguably the most versatile medium. You can paint on most surfaces including paper, wood and fabric. You can paint in most styles from watercolour-like glazes to thick impasto. You can use it for creating collages, where the paint itself provides not only colour and texture but adhesion as well.

During the many years I have been painting landscapes with acrylics, I have developed techniques that overcome all the 'problems' listed above. It is an approach based on a watercolourist's need to work quickly and directly.

I have included advice on composition, colours and perspective for landscape painting, as well as a chapter on how changing seasons affect a landscape. I do hope you find the contents of this section useful and inspiring.

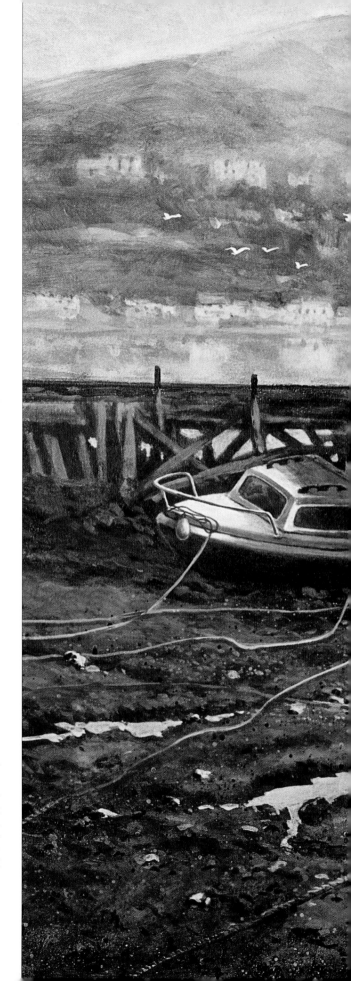

Teignmouth Harbour
51 x 41cm (20 x 16in)

The subject (the boat) dominates the composition in this painting. Pools of water in the low tide mud provide not only a lead-in through to the background, but also an area at the bottom of the painting where the light, reflected sky tones can be introduced. The position of the mooring ropes was altered to strengthen the lead-in effect. Splatter and glazing techniques were used to give the foreground interest, form and texture.

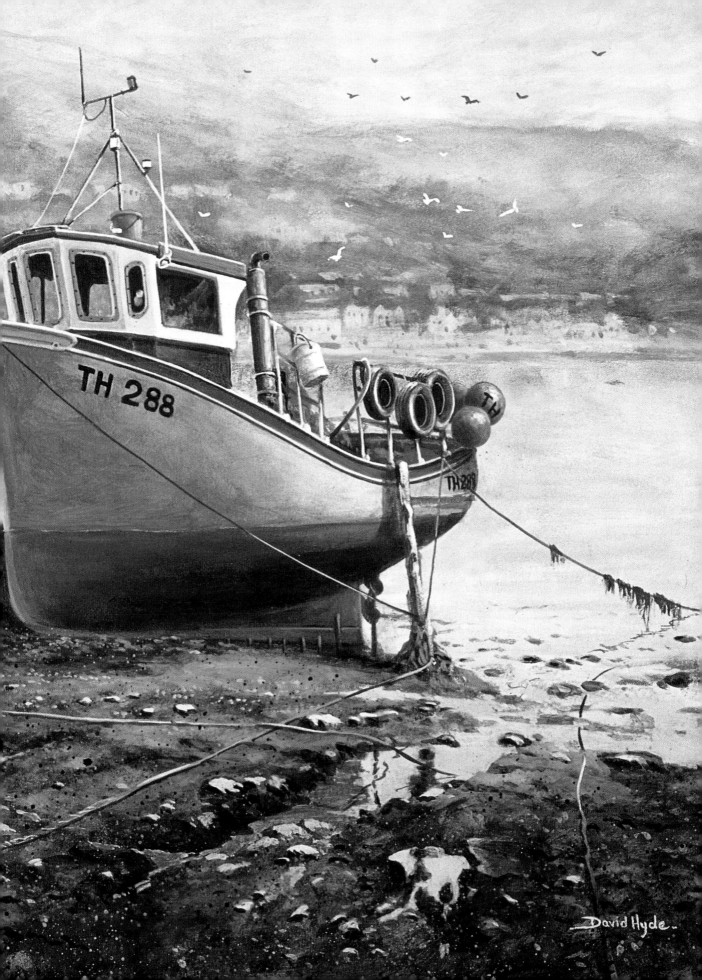

Composition

Composition is more important than drawing. I use charcoal because it stops you getting too distracted with detail. You can rough in your composition very quickly but do stand back and look at it long and hard before proceeding. If something is wrong, you can quickly correct it. If you have spent a couple of hours on your drawing, you are less inclined to make any alterations. Do not worry about detail; you can put this in with paint later.

Consider for a moment a still-life painting; a real classic with fruit in a bowl, a wine bottle and half-filled wine glass and perhaps a few walnuts and vine leaves in the foreground. Now ask yourself – did the artist come upon this scene by accident and decide to paint it? No, of course not. Something, perhaps the fruit in the bowl, would have been the initial inspiration and the other items were added to create a picture. This selection of objects and their placement relative to one another is called composition, and composition is important in all paintings.

You may be thinking that surely landscape is different. You can move a wine bottle but you cannot move a church; you can arrange a vine leaf but a river is fixed in position. Well, not only is it possible to rearrange a landscape, but artists have been doing it for years. Mentally select objects from the scene in front of you and place them in your painting to create a composition. You need not select everything and you are quite at liberty to alter or even add objects to create the effect you want. This is known as artistic licence and your paintings will look all the better for it.

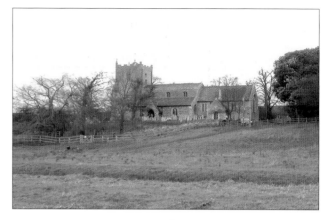

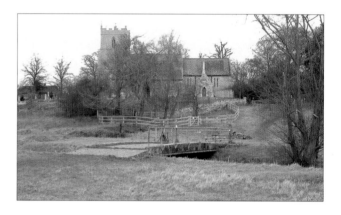

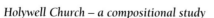

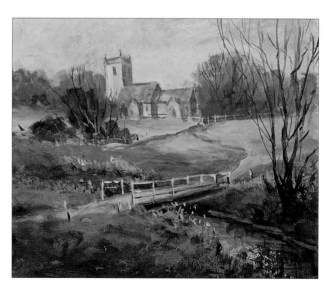

Holywell Church – a compositional study

In the middle photograph the church is obscured by trees. For a clearer view, the photograph above needed to be taken from across the bridge and to the right. In the resulting study, I reduced the size of the obscuring trees and added the church detail using the second photograph. Additionally, the existing footpath was emphasised to link the bridge and the church, strengthening the composition.

Golden section

When you look at any picture, your eyes will scan most often the areas one-third in from the edges. So, as an artist, you can 'guide' your viewer's eye to rest more easily on the focal point by placing it one-third of the way in from any edge. This placement is known as the 'rule of thirds'. There are four points where the vertical and horizontal thirds cross, which is called the golden section. By placing your focal point in the golden section (see example), its strength in the painting is bolstered.

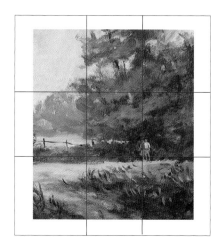

The two figures in this study are small but become a strong focal point when placed on a golden section.

Focal point

The focal point of a picture can be the subject, part of the subject, a bright colour or a dramatic contrast in tone. Whatever it happens to be, the eye must naturally return to it and be able to rest. Have only one focal point or the picture will seem confused. If human figures are included, even if they are quite small, our brains accord them more importance than their size warrants and they can, even unintentionally, become the focal point of the painting. This is also true, though less so, of animals. They must strengthen the focal point and not distract from it.

Eye level

I live on the edge of the Fens in Cambridgeshire where the horizon is mostly visible and not obscured by hills or mountains, but usually the horizon line will be hidden. You still need to know where it is and where to place it in your painting. This can seem a difficult task but you just need to think of an imaginary line at your eye level. To determine the eye level from where you are standing or sitting, look straight ahead and move your head from side to side. Represent this imaginary line with an actual mark on your painting board. Where you place this mark is up to you, but keep the golden section in mind for your focal point. One-third from the top or bottom of the board can be a good start. A low horizon line adds drama to tall objects such as trees and high buildings. If you choose a horizon line in the middle, beware of cutting the painting in two and making the picture look static, unless you are deliberately trying to create a feeling of peace and tranquillity. A high horizon line will focus interest on the foreground to mid-distance. Do not be afraid to let tall objects disappear out of the top of your picture.

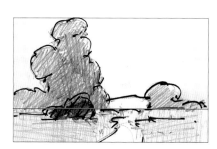

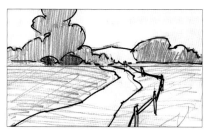

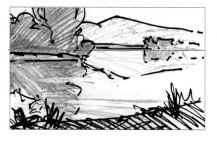

The three sketches show from top to bottom: low, middle and high eye level.

L-shaped composition

An L-shaped composition has a strong upright element, often a tree, placed
on or near a vertical third and a strong level element placed on or near a
horizontal third. The focal point, meanwhile, can be placed near the opposite
vertical third. The upright is dominant but never the focal point. The bottom
section of the 'L' should lift the viewer's eye up into the picture. This can be
achieved with some close-up vegetation or even a strong shadow across the
picture, below the bottom third.

River Scene
*The jetty and the tree make up the L-shape
in this composition.*

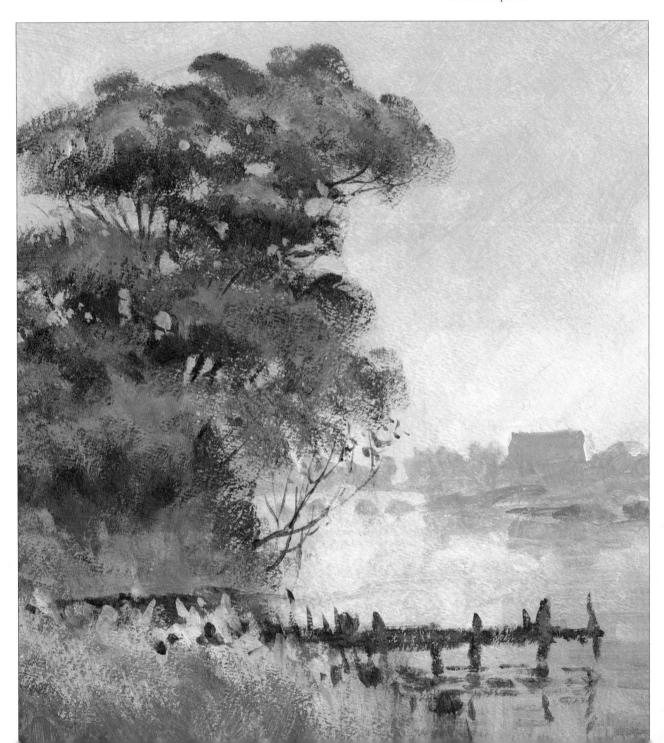

U-shaped composition

Similar to the 'L' but with a second, normally less strong, vertical used on the opposite third. This gives a more enclosed feeling to the painting and is often used in woodland or street scenes. The two verticals act as a frame to the focal point, which can now be placed nearer to the centre of the picture. Again, the bottom section of the 'U' should lift the viewer's eye up into the picture.

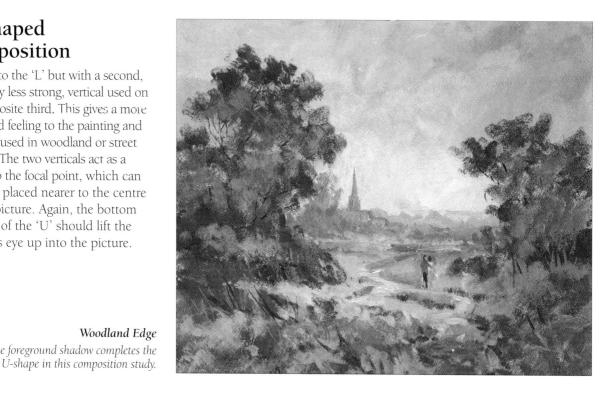

Woodland Edge
The foreground shadow completes the U-shape in this composition study.

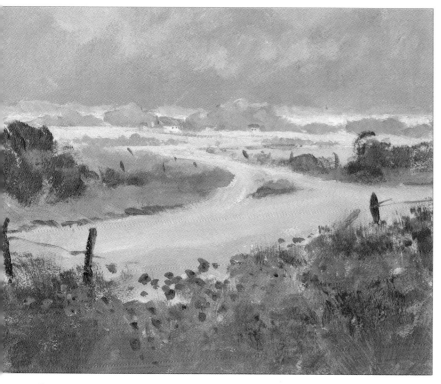

S-shaped composition

An S-shaped composition will give a more open feeling to a picture and can be used when painting scenes that lack vertical trees or buildings, such as mountain or beach scenes. The 'S' shape can take an obvious form, like a road or stream leading your eye in and around the painting. Or it can be subtler, using field edges, different areas of landscape colour or cloud shadows to form a pattern that leads the eye. The focal point can now be placed on a third or any of the golden points.

Landscape with Poppies
The S-shaped road leads the eye through this picture.

Colours for landscape

You can paint a picture with just three primary colours, because from these you can mix a version of all others. The only addition is white to control the tones. Most artists use a palette based on three or more of each of the primaries to give themselves a greater range when mixing. A useful, basic palette is listed below.

Yellows

Lemon yellow A bright, sunshine yellow. It adds warmth to whites and freshness to greens.

Naples yellow A non-insistent yellow that can lighten tones and add softness to many mixes.

Raw sienna A 'must-have' colour. The dull yellow is useful for grass greens, brickwork and so on.

Reds

Cadmium red A useful bright red. Warms up mixes wonderfully.

Cadmium orange A versatile colour – good for sunsets, sunny brickwork, toning greens and much else.

Burnt sienna Another vital colour, a dull red or warm orange brown with many uses.

Burnt umber Use sparingly. Mix with phthalocyanine blue to make a lovely deep green.

Blues

French ultramarine A most versatile, warm blue, useful for making greys and distant greens.

Phthalocyanine blue (phthalo blue) A strong, cool blue which is good for skies but most useful in making greens.

Cerulean blue A good soft, sky blue. Useful for distant shadows and for mixing soft greens.

Useful secondaries

Chromium oxide green A useful base for many green mixes and a good unifying colour to use all over a picture.

Dioxazine purple Great for underpainting shadow areas. Good in shadows and grey mixes.

Whites

Titanium white You will need plenty of this white for mixing with and toning in all colours.

Mixing greens

In my basic list of paints I have included a useful, general purpose green. However, if you are a beginner, I would suggest locking away any green you may have for the time being; the temptation to reach for it in times of crisis will be too strong. We all know that blue and yellow make green, but there is much, much more to it than that!

Add white to the mixes below to vary the tone. However, adding white can make greens look too cool and minty. If so, substitute Naples yellow to warm up your greens.

Grass greens

Spring grass
Lemon yellow + phthalo blue

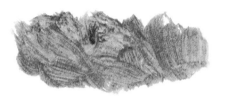

Summer grass
French ultramarine + lemon yellow

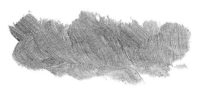

Autumn/winter grass
Cerulean blue + raw sienna

Tree greens

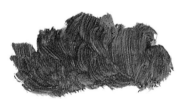

Summer trees
Phthalo blue + a little burnt sienna

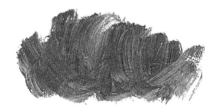

Autumn trees
Burnt sienna + a little phthalo blue

Spring/winter trees
French ultramarine + burnt sienna. For spring trees overpaint with small amounts of yellow-green to suggest new growth – see page 52.

Colour and tone

Now we have discussed mixing, we ought to clarify the difference between colour and tone. Red, blue, green, purple and so on are colours: degrees of lightness and darkness of that colour are called tone. This sounds simple enough and in the monochrome example shown, painted only in burnt sienna (plus white to control tone), it is easy to see that all the elements of light, shade, foreground and distance are perfectly readable.

In most paintings where you use many colours, you have to judge the tone of each colour against the tone of the different colours and tones in the picture. If you have a digital camera, you can quickly assess the tones in your painting as a whole. Take its picture and remove the colour, making it either sepia or black and white. Your painting should still look 'correct'. The elements should still appear in their proper place. After all, many of us watched black and white television quite happily for years. Being able to alter the tone of a colour is more important than mixing different hues.

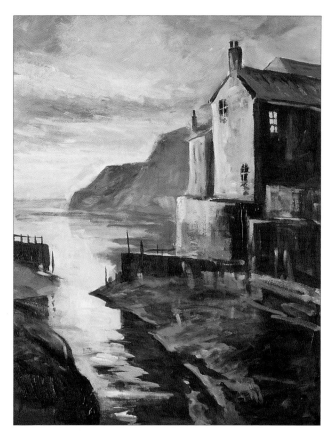

Evening Low Tide
A monochrome study painted in only burnt sienna and white.

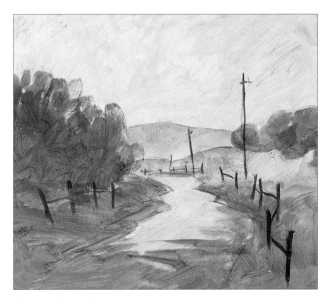

Country Lane
A tonal underpainting painted in raw sienna, burnt sienna and dioxazine purple.

Tonal underpainting

An underpainting is a very useful thing and has three functions. On a practical level, the underpainting will seal the drawing, which is particularly important with charcoal. It will also cover the whiteness of the board, which is handy when painting in the sunshine, and it makes it a lot easier to judge tonal values as you paint.

I use three colours: raw sienna to establish the light areas, raw sienna mixed with burnt sienna for general distance and mid-distance tones, and burnt sienna for foreground tones. Dioxazine purple can be added to all mixes to indicate areas of darker shadow. Mix your colours with medium to make them transparent and you will not lose your drawing detail. There is no need to use white as the whiteness of the board will show through the transparent paint. Leave to dry thoroughly.

Creating depth

In landscape painting, we are trying to represent the three-dimensional scene in front of us on a two-dimensional board. The scene will have some objects close to us, some a little further away and so on until we come to the most distant objects we can see. The illusion of distance needs to be created in our paintings. If done successfully, it will give our pictures depth.

Linear perspective

The further away from us an object is, the smaller it will appear. A straight line of telegraph poles going away from us would appear to get smaller and smaller. This effect is known as linear perspective, commonly referred to just as perspective. If the line of telegraph poles were long enough, they would eventually seem to disappear at a point on the horizon called the 'vanishing point'. In landscape these effects are drawn with a pencil or charcoal line. Look at the line drawing on the right to see how linear perspective creates the illusion of depth.

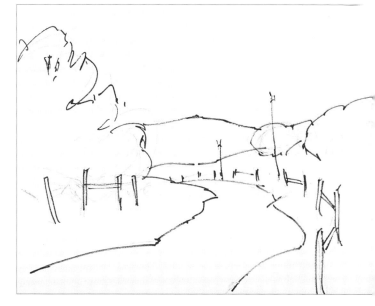

Country Lane
A study in linear perspective.

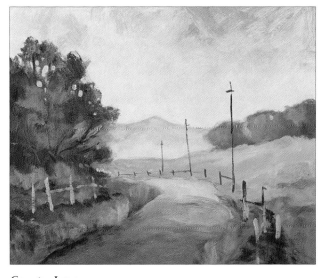

Country Lane
An study in aerial perspective.

Aerial perspective

Tone will also be affected by distance. The further away an object is, the lighter, less detailed and less contrasting its tone will appear. This can be achieved simply by adding white to your mixes, and reducing the amount of detail. You can paint dark colours in the distance, but they must be lighter than the equivalent foreground darks. This recession of tone, contrast and detail is caused by water droplets and pollutants in the atmosphere, and is known to artists as aerial perspective. If you can successfully combine linear and aerial perspective, you will create a true feeling of depth.

Seasons

Spring
30.5 x 25cm (12 x 9¾in)

The use of cerulean blue and Naples yellow gives the sky tones a spring freshness. This is echoed by the use of lemon yellow with a touch of phthalo blue in the grass on the foreground riverbank. The trees and bushes will lack a full covering of leaves and can be painted in warmer winter tree tones. Small amounts of light yellow-green randomly brushed over will suggest the new spring growth.

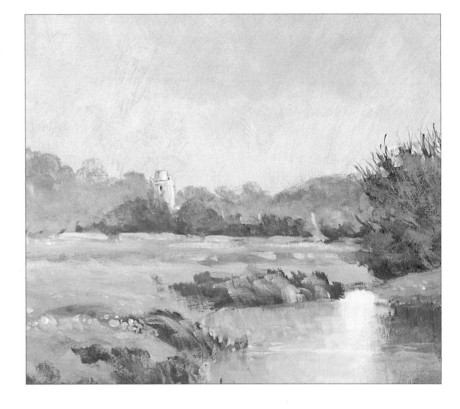

Summer
30.5 x 25cm (12 x 9¾in)

An overall increase in contrast will help suggest those rich summer landscapes. A deeper, warm sky has been mixed using French ultramarine and a little cadmium red. Summer clouds have been used to keep the sky from becoming too oppressive and to give a light background to the distant trees. Be careful not to overdo the greens. Distant trees can be painted using French ultramarine, raw sienna and white, while the closer trees on the right can be mixed using phthalo blue, burnt sienna and Naples yellow. A richer green of French ultramarine and lemon yellow with white can be used in the foreground grasses. The use of the burnt sienna tone in the left foreground breaks up the green and adds a warm richness to the painting.

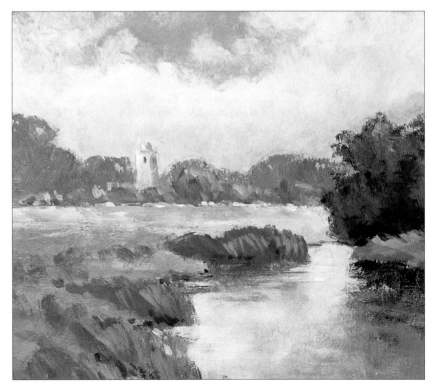

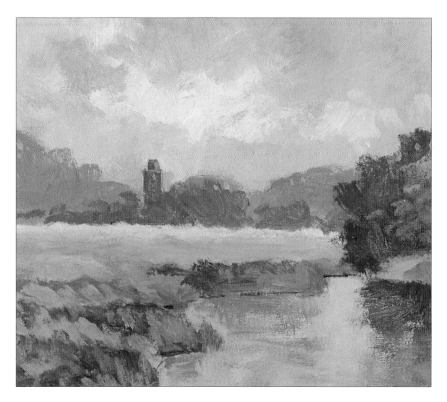

Autumn
30.5 x 25cm (12 x 9¾in)

The reds and golds have been kept under control here to avoid garishness. In this study I have warmed the painting overall by using cadmium orange in the sky mix. Cerulean blue mixed with cadmium orange together with plenty of titanium white makes lovely warm, grey clouds. There are still greens in the landscape but they now lack the richness of summer. Mix them with cerulean blue and raw sienna or lemon yellow and lighten the mix with titanium white. The autumn trees are mixed from burnt sienna with a small amount of phthalo blue. Add white to control tone and add more white to paint the distant trees. Raw sienna and titanium white are used to suggest the waterside reeds dying back.

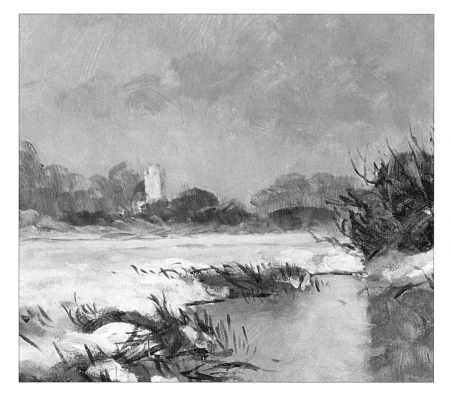

Winter
30.5 x 25cm (12 x 9¾in)

No landscape book would be complete without a snow scene. The sky and river tones are darker than much of the landscape in this study. I have used a similar mix to the summer sky but strengthened the tone a little. All the foliage is now painted with various greys, browns and ochres using mixes of French ultramarine, cerulean blue, raw sienna, burnt sienna and either titanium white or Naples yellow to lighten, replacing the green tones of the seasons before. Do not just paint the snow white. Add blues into the distance and areas of shadow. Naples yellow and small amounts of cadmium red or orange can be used in the sunny areas. The brightest snow in the foreground can be highlighted with white and a touch of lemon yellow.

Distant Mountains

On holiday on the Isle of Skye, Scotland, I took many landscape photographs like the one shown below. As with so many snapshots, the wide angle camera lens can diminish the effect of the mountains. The painting was created from this photograph using the road running to the left as a useful lead-in, increasing the mid-distance and making more of the mountains behind. This recreates the feeling of the scene that has been lost in the photograph. This composition is S-shaped.

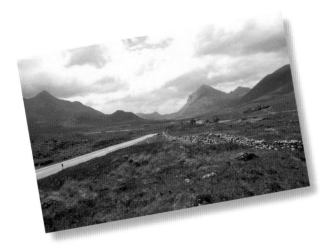

This photograph has all the basic elements for creating a Highland landscape. Note that the road needs some artistic license to make it work in a painting.

You will need
Primed board, 46 x 36cm
(18 x 14¼in)
Charcoal
Acrylic medium
Titanium white
Raw sienna
Naples yellow
Lemon yellow
Cadmium red
Burnt sienna
Phthalo blue
Cerulean blue
Chromium oxide green
Dioxazine purple
Rubber-tipped colour shaper
Brushes:
    No. 4, no. 6 and no.10 flat
    Rigger
    Fan

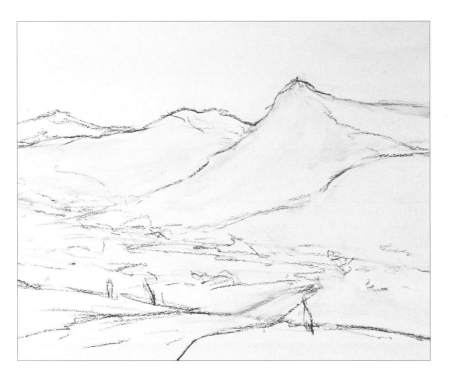

1. Use charcoal to sketch in the mountains on your primed board. Work quickly and concentrate on the composition. The beauty of charcoal is that it can be changed or rubbed away easily using a wet sponge, so try to be free and expressive with your marks.

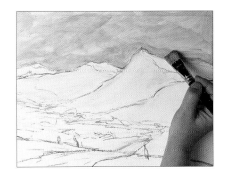

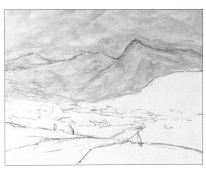

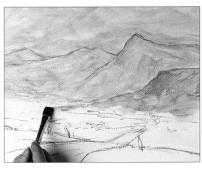

2. Mix medium with a little water and some raw sienna. Block in the sky using a no.10 flat brush. When you reach the top of the mountains, run your brush into the charcoal to seal it.

3. Add a touch of dioxazine purple to your paint mix and block in the mountains. Make brush strokes that follow the shape of the mountains, but keep them loose. The main objective is to cover up all of the white.

4. Add more purple to your paint mix and, using the no. 6 flat brush, block in the nearest mountain with brush strokes that follow the contours of your drawing. Using a fresh mix of medium and raw sienna, block in the mid-distance.

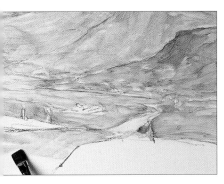

5. Use medium and raw sienna to block in the nearest section of path, as shown.

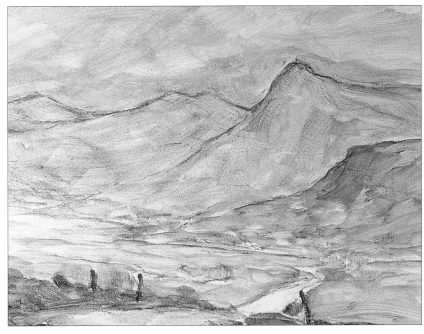

6. Add a pale purple shadow to the beginning of the road to lead the eye into the landscape. Paint the foreground grasses with burnt sienna. Make sure paint has been applied over all of the charcoal marks. This will seal the drawing. Allow to dry.

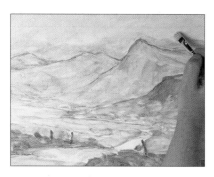

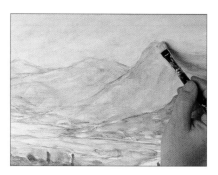

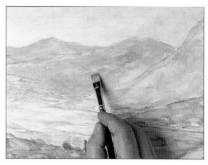

7. On your palette, add cerulean blue and a touch of Naples yellow to titanium white. Keep this pale blue mix fairly opaque; add very little water. Now block in the sky with the no.10 flat brush.

8. With the paint that is left on the bristles, dry brush over the mountains. Clean and dry the brush, then mix white and Naples yellow and paint a yellow haze above the mountains. Bring the yellow paint just over the top of the mountains to soften the edges and push them into the distance.

9. Make a mix of dioxazine purple, cerulean blue and Naples yellow to match the tone of the sky. Using the no. 6 flat brush, paint in the most distant mountain. Add more blue to the mix and paint the neighbouring mountain. Use a clean, damp brush to lift off small areas of paint where light hits the mountains.

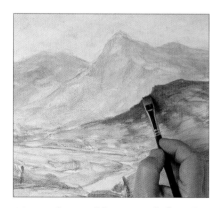

10. With your blue mix, darken the top but not the front of the third mountain. Now add burnt sienna to the mix and strengthen the colour on the last mountain. Dry-brush the tops of both mountains to soften the colour.

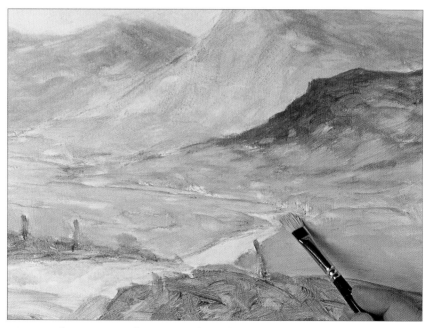

11. Mix chromium oxide green and Naples yellow with a small amount of titanium white to make a subtle green. Block in the middle distance and take the green slightly over the bottom of the mountains.

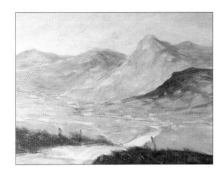

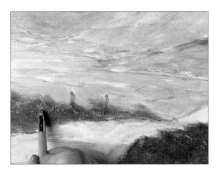

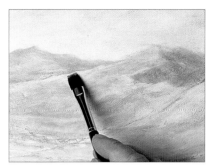

12. Using a mix of lemon yellow, burnt sienna and phthalo blue with a touch of dioxazine purple, roughly paint in the areas of foreground on either side of the path.

13. Before the foreground dries, use the rubber-tipped colour shaper to lift off small areas of paint. This will create the texture of foliage.

14. Use lemon yellow and cadmium red mixed with plenty of white to add highlights where the sunshine hits the third mountain with the no. 6 flat brush. Now dry brush the same mix where the sunlight catches the edge of the mountain range.

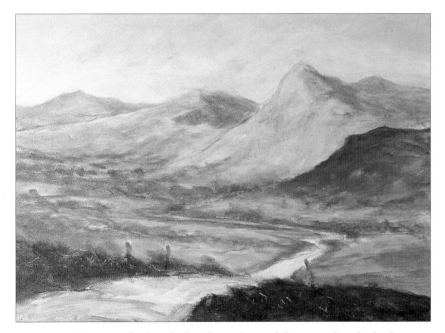

15. Using the no. 4 flat brush, break up the middle ground with shadows using a mid-tone green mixed from chromium oxide green, dioxazine purple and Naples yellow. Vary the proportions in the mix to create a range of shadows from bluish green to purplish green. Tone down the purple of the nearest mountain with a mid-tone green.

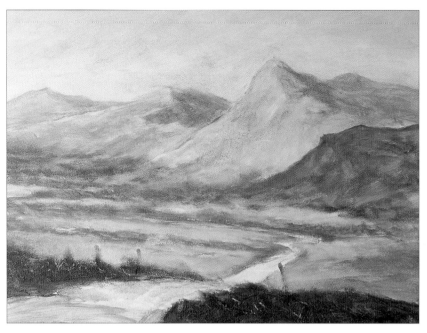

16. To make the middle ground look as though it is bathed in soft sunlight, add highlights with the no. 6 flat brush, using a mix of white and lemon yellow. Soften the nearest mountain with a purplish green.

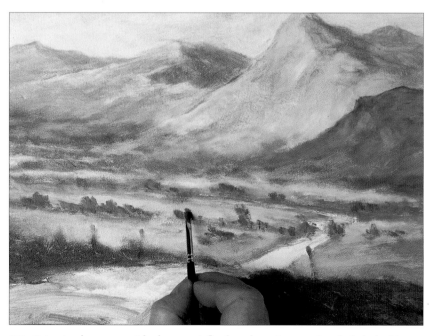

17. Paint in the trees with the no. 4 flat brush, using a mix of phthalo blue, burnt sienna and Naples yellow.

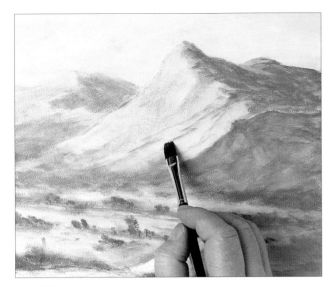

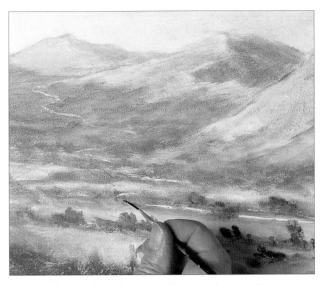

18. With the no. 6 flat brush, use a mix of cerulean blue, dioxazine purple and raw sienna to darken the tops of the mountains. Bring a suggestion of shadows down the front of the third mountain.

19. Add a touch of lemon yellow to white and use a rigger brush to paint the road meandering away into the distance. Paint a delicate, broken line to achieve this effect.

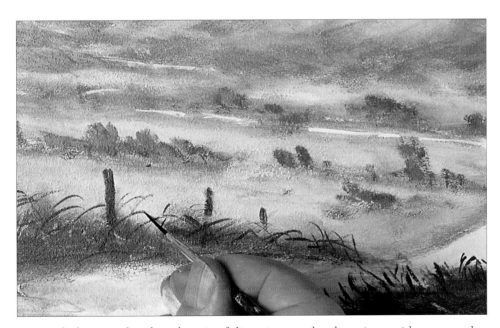

20. With the rigger brush and a mix of dioxazine purple, chromium oxide green and burnt sienna, add blades of long grass in upright strokes. Strengthen the fence posts using the same mix.

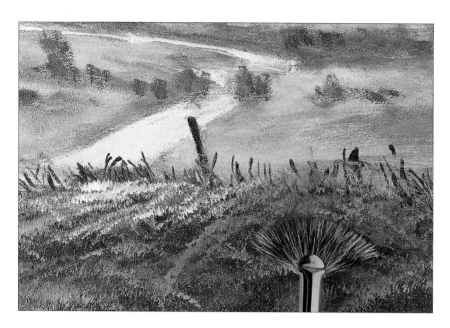

21. Use a fan brush to add highlights where sunlight catches the top of the heather. Create some highlights with pure white and others with various mixes of dioxazine purple, cadmium red and lemon yellow.

22. Add definition to the side of the road with a mix of burnt sienna and dioxazine purple, using the no.10 flat brush. Add medium and glaze in the shadow falling across the start of the road.

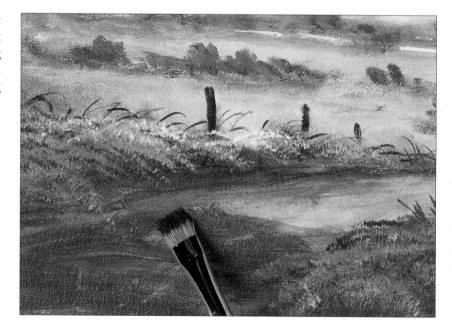

Do not be afraid to alter aspects of your painting even at quite a late stage. I felt the mountain needed more definition so I changed the shape slightly using a mix of dioxazine purple, chromium oxide green and cadmium red with a no. 6 flat brush.

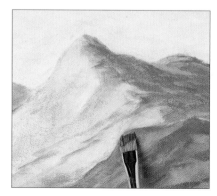

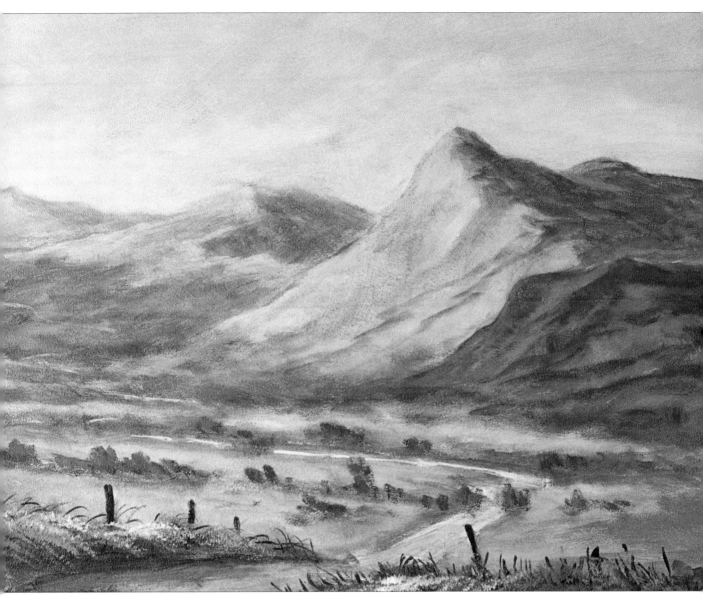

The finished painting.

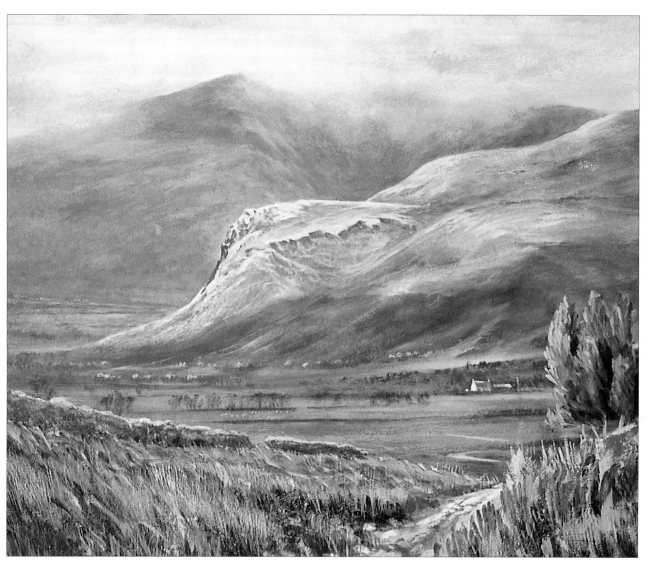

After the Storm, Cumbria
51 x 41cm (20 x 16¼in)

I saw this subject while driving in Cumbria. The sun was spotlighting the landscape through a gap in the storm clouds. The cloud and the patch of sunlight were moving quickly and by the time I stopped the car and grabbed my camera, the sun had moved too much to the left. I took the picture anyway and put the sunshine back in the 'correct' place when I did the painting.

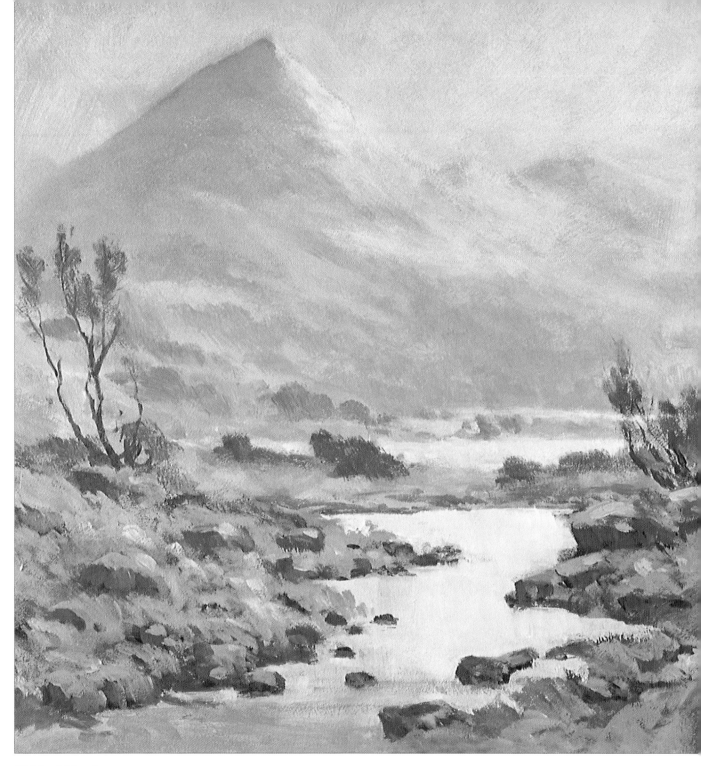

Highland Morning
33 x 36cm (13 x 14¼in)

Naples yellow has been used extensively in the colour mixes to suggest a low morning light cast across this landscape from the right. More has been made of the small brook to create a lead-in and provide a useful area to bring light into the lower part of the painting. I darkened the tops of mountains to emphasise their scale. Notice also how there is low contrast in the background, and higher contrast in the foreground. This is aerial perspective and its use will strengthen the effect of depth.

Still Water

This early morning scene photographed in my home town of St. Ives, Cambridgeshire, shows the River Great Ouse with almost no flow, providing some wonderful reflections of the church and distant riverbank. The church spire, the old mill building to the left and the foreground bushes make a useful composition group. The only small alterations I made were to widen the river slightly on the left and add to the floating weed to provide a stronger lead-in.

You will need

Primed board, 46 x 36cm
  (18 x 14¼in)
Charcoal
Acrylic medium
Titanium white
Raw sienna
Naples yellow
Lemon yellow
Burnt sienna
Burnt umber
Phthalo blue
Cerulean blue
Chromium oxide green
Dioxazine purple
Rubber-tipped colour shaper
Brushes:
  No. 6 and no.10 flat
  No. 4 round
  Rigger

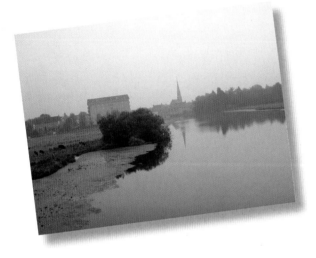

This view of St. Ives is from the bypass bridge. It is always worth a look upriver from this position. On this occasion the still water gave the town an air of peace and tranquillity.

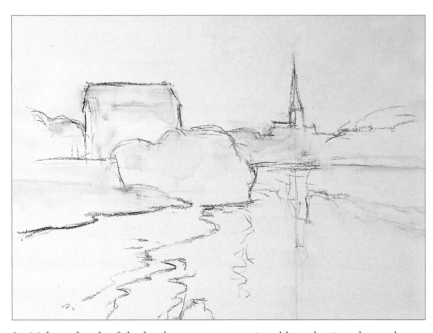

1. Make a sketch of the landscape on your primed board using charcoal.

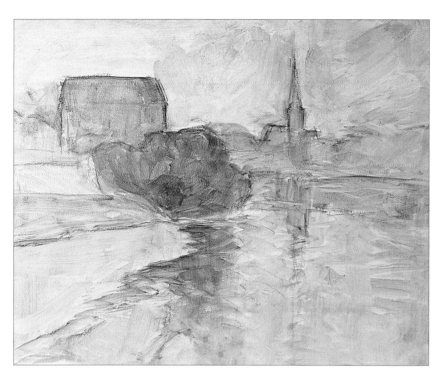

2. Use the no. 10 flat brush and raw sienna mixed with medium to underpaint the sky, the meadow, the duckweed and reflections in the water. Then mix raw sienna and dioxazine purple to block in the buildings and their reflections. Add a touch of raw sienna to burnt sienna and underpaint the bush and its reflection. When your undercoat is dry, paint a shadow in dioxazine purple at the base of the bush and bring the colour down into the reflection. Make sure the charcoal marks are covered and leave to dry.

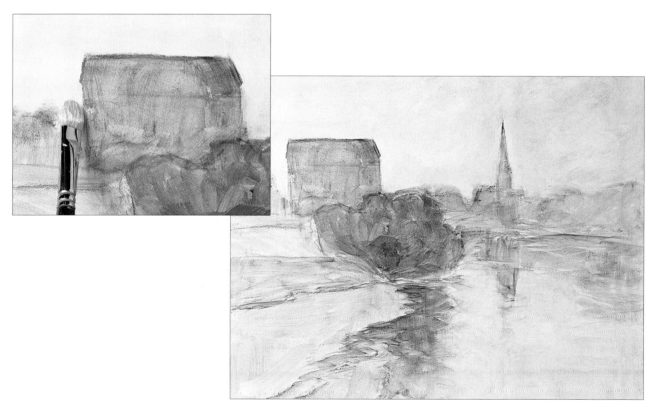

3. Use a mix of titanium white and Naples yellow to soften the sky and define the edges of the buildings. Then bring the same mix down through the reflections on the water.

65

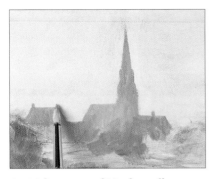

4. Make a mix of Naples yellow, dioxazine purple and a touch of cerulean blue. Add a little water to create a morning mist over the mill and the bushes to its left. Change to a no. 4 round brush when painting the spire.

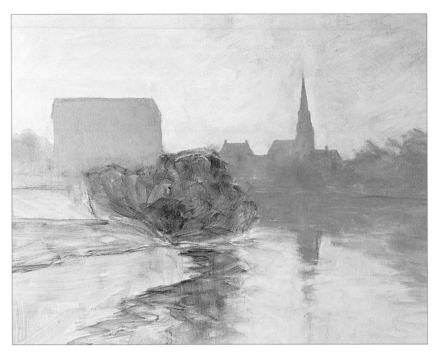

5. Now block in the church and surrounding bushes in a uniform tone. Then add the reflection, painting a broken reflection of the spire. Use the same mix and brushes as in step 4 but less diluted than before.

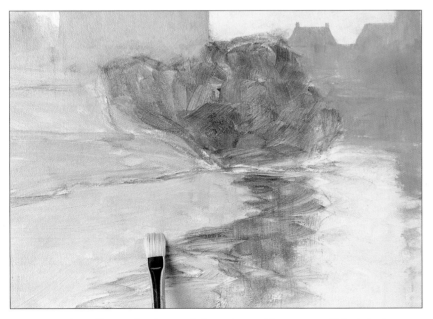

6. Mix Naples yellow with white and chromium oxide green and block in the banks on the left-hand side with the no. 6 flat brush. Naples yellow warms the green and, being a soft colour, is also good for distance.

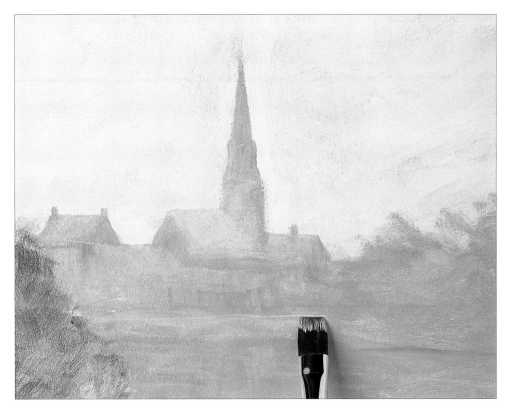

7. Mix some cerulean blue with titanium white to suggest the roofs of the buildings.

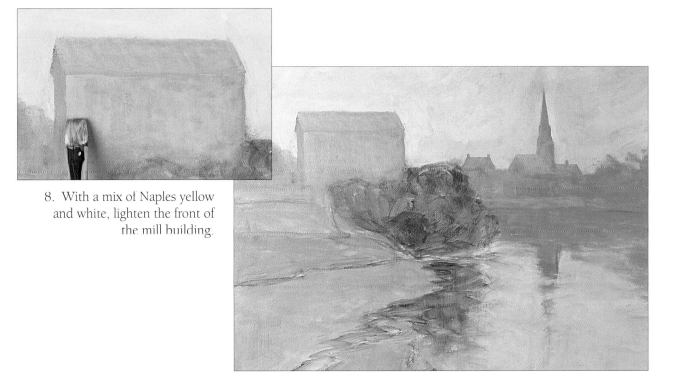

8. With a mix of Naples yellow and white, lighten the front of the mill building.

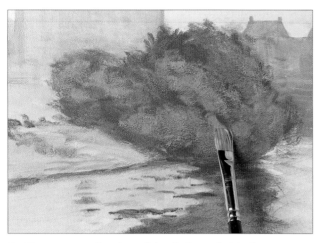

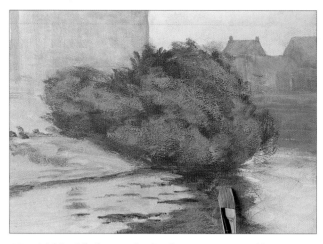

9. You now need to knock back the red. Mix burnt umber with chromium oxide green and paint the bush, allowing areas of the burnt sienna underpainting to show through. Work into the reflection forming the edge of the duckweed.

10. Add highlights to the bush using a mix of lemon yellow, white and chromium oxide green.

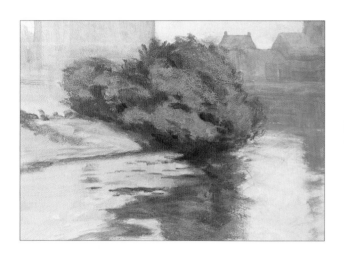

11. Strengthen the shadow beneath the bush using a mix of phthalo blue, burnt umber and raw sienna.

12. Using a mix of raw sienna, chromium oxide green and white, scumble across in front of the mill to create distant trees. Using a mix of raw sienna and chromium oxide green with less white than the previous mix, scrumble in the bankside vegetation until it meets the bottom of the bush.

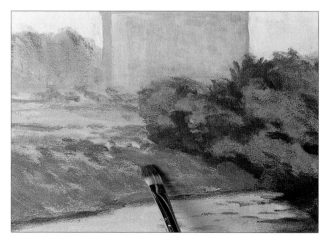

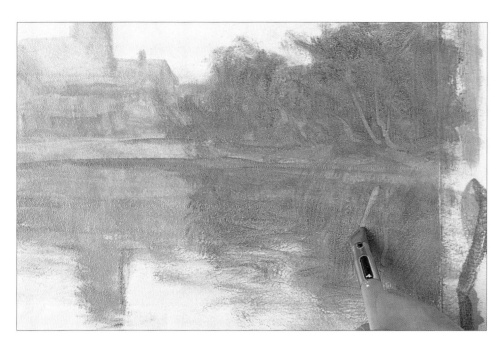

13. Add dioxazine purple to the first mix you used in step 12. Add water to make a wetter mix and give shape to the bush on the right by building up the shadows. Before the paint dries, use the rubber-tipped colour shaper to suggest reflections.

14. Using a mix of cerulean blue and white and a no. 4 round brush, add small dots to suggest holes in the top of the bushes.

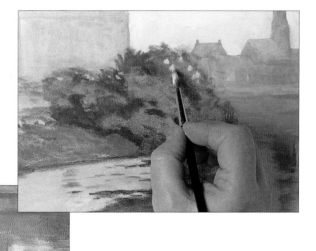

15. With the no. 6 flat brush, introduce some blue into the water using the same mix, slightly diluted.

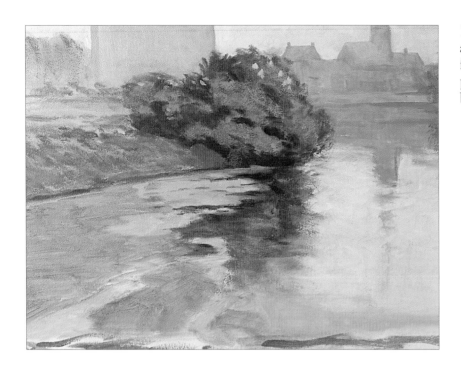

16. To create a shadow falling across the duckweed in the foreground, mix cerulean blue, phthalo blue and raw sienna and block in the area shown.

17. Using the rigger brush and a fairly watery mix of white and Naples yellow, paint some light branches on the bush. Then with a mix of burnt sienna, phthalo blue and raw sienna, paint darker branches and twigs poking out of the bush. Paint them all with quick, confident movements. When dry, tone down some of the paler branches with a shadowy glaze of cerulean blue.

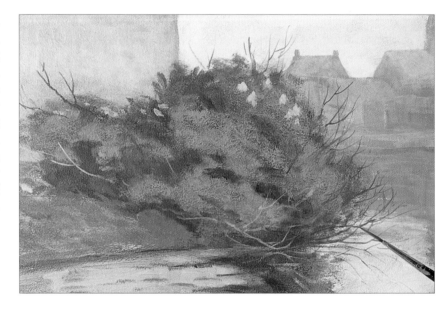

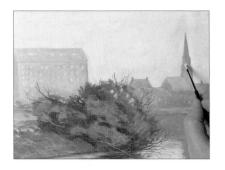

18. With the no. 4 round brush and a mix of white, cerulean blue and a touch of purple, add details such as windows and the church clock. Ensure there is not too much contrast within each building.

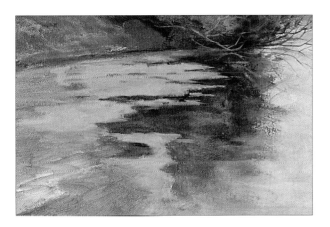

19. Finally, suggest sunlight on the duckweed using a mixture of lemon yellow and a tiny spot of phthalo blue.

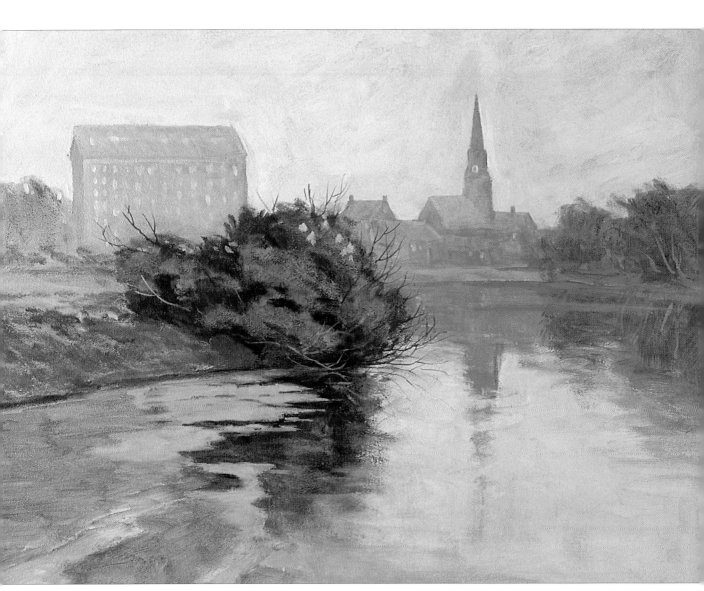

The finished painting.

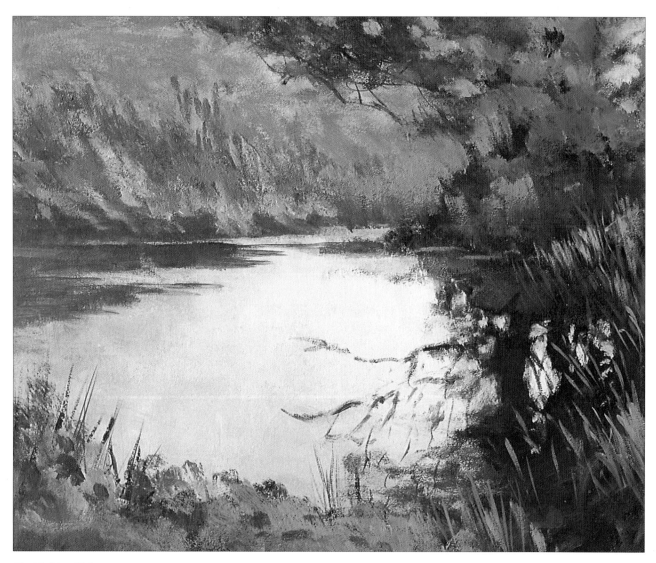

The Fishing Hole
30.5 x 25cm (12 x 9¾in)

This loose, simple study of still water is strengthened by selecting a high eye level. The only sky in the painting is within the reflection in the water, thus giving this picture an interesting 'upside-down' feeling. We can see that the water is still by the more defined reflection of the tree to the right. Avoid an exact mirror image as this can look a little false.

River Great Ouse at Hemingford Grey
30.5 x 23cm (12 x 9in)

I live near this river and love to include water in my paintings. Water, even if it is only in the form of puddles, allows you to bring down the sky tones, giving more opportunity to create patterns by using light and reflection. Note the soft reflection under the buildings compared to the harder rippled reflection in the foreground. This adds perspective to the river.

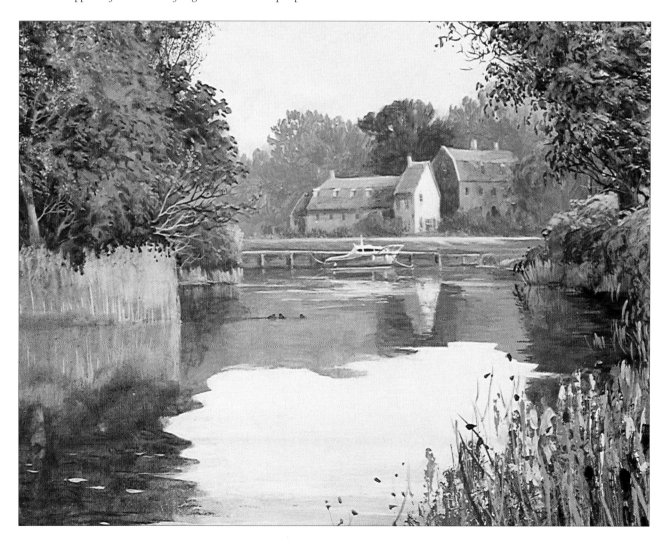

Ancient Tree

Trees can often make interesting subjects in their own right. This old ivy-covered tree is a case in point. The photograph is too cluttered and needs simplifying to create a successful composition. The farm buildings in the background are too distracting so I left them out. The ground was sloping and I emphasised this slope in the right-hand foreground. The fence and gate were simplified and I made the path through it clearer to provide a lead-in. There are one or two smaller trees in the photograph which again, to avoid confusion, I simply left out.

You will need
Primed board, 46 x 36cm
  (18 x 14¼in)
Charcoal
Titanium white
Raw sienna
Naples yellow
Cadmium red
Burnt sienna
Burnt umber
Phthalo blue
French ultramarine
Chromium oxide green
Dioxazine purple
Natural sponge
Brushes:
  No. 6 and no. 10 flat
  No. 4 round
  Rigger
  Bungee brush

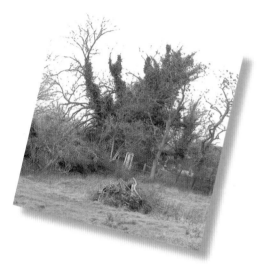

I normally carry a camera in my painting bag. Trees standing out on their own are worth recording and can often make paintings in their own right.

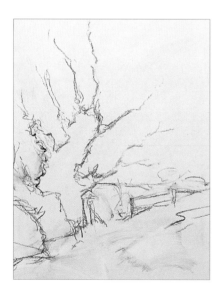

1. Draw a charcoal sketch of your picture on your primed board.

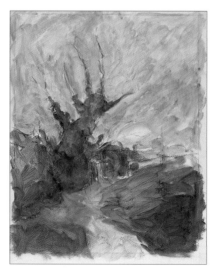

2. With the no. 10 flat brush, paint an underpainting using raw sienna for the light areas, dioxazine purple for the shadows and burnt sienna and purple for the mid-tones.

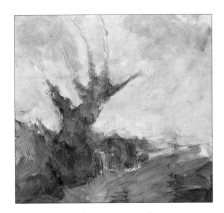

3. Mixing white with cadmium red and French ultramarine makes a slightly mauve grey. Vary the warmth of the sky by using different proportions of these colours as you paint.

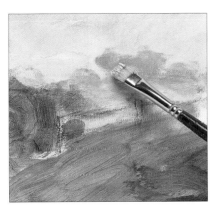

4. Using the no. 6 flat brush, paint in distant trees with a mix of French ultramarine, Naples yellow and white.

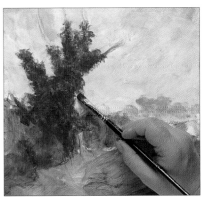

5. Paint in the tree trunk using a mix of phthalo blue, burnt umber and a touch of Naples yellow. Before it dries, scumble around the edges with a dry brush to create the impression of ivy leaves.

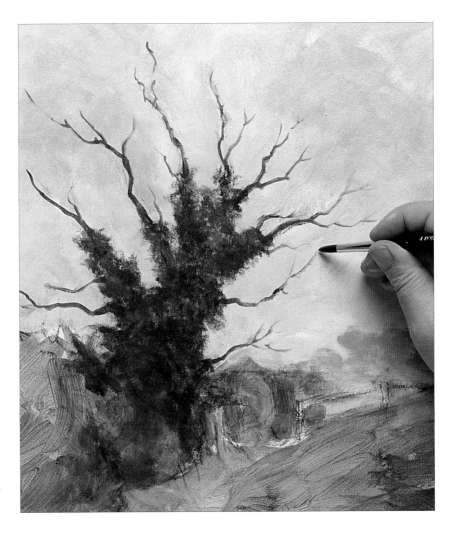

6. Water down the same mix and, with a no. 4 round brush, paint in the branches.

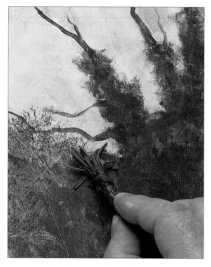

7. Use the bungee brush (or the sponge) to spread colour outwards. Press the brush into quite a wet area of paint and, working quickly, push it out towards the sky, twisting it as you go.

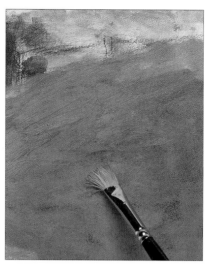

8. Using the no. 6 flat brush, roughly paint a mix of chromium oxide green and Naples yellow over the two banks in the foreground. Leave areas of the underpainting showing through.

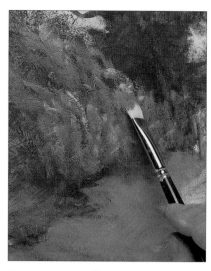

9. Use a mix of burnt sienna and Naples yellow to create the impression of light in the hedgerow. Work from the bottom of the hedgerow upwards, mixing lighter shades as you go.

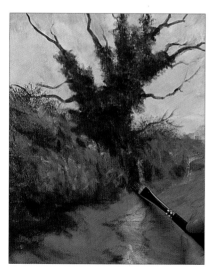

10. Use a mix of phthalo blue, burnt umber with a touch of Naples yellow to add shadow to the bottom of the hedgerow.

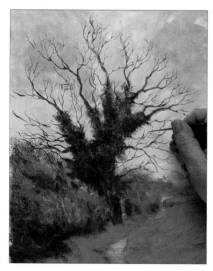

11. Make a watery mix of French ultramarine and burnt sienna. Using a rigger brush, add the finer branches and twigs to the tree.

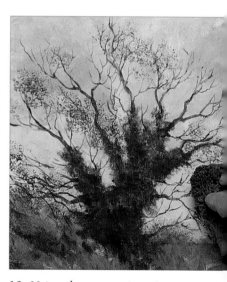

12. Using the same mix as in step 11, lightly sponge in some remaining winter leaves.

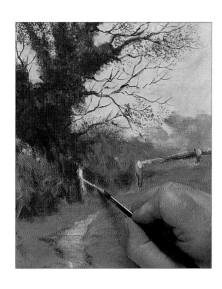

13. Use the no. 4 round brush to add fence posts. Mix burnt umber and French ultramarine for the dark parts of the fence and burnt umber and white for the lighter parts.

14. Mix a pale green using chromium oxide green, raw sienna and white and brush over the ivy with a no. 6 flat brush.

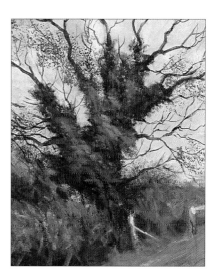

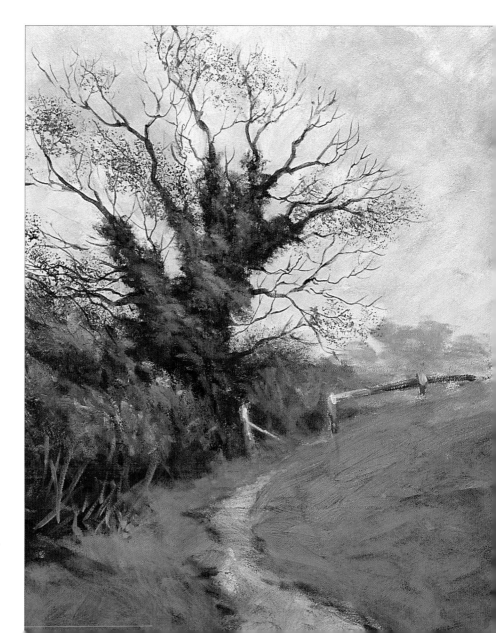

The finished painting.

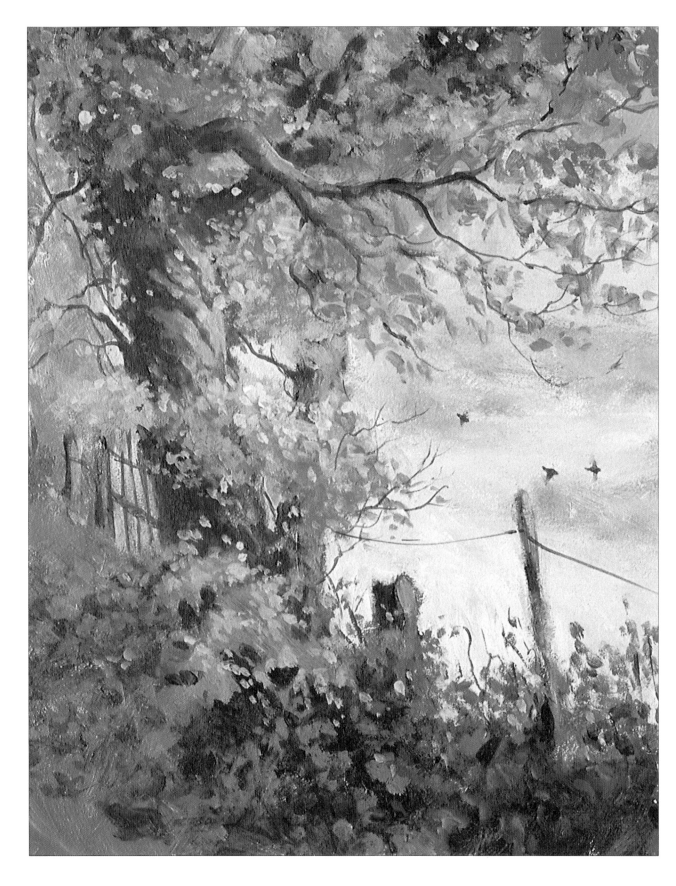

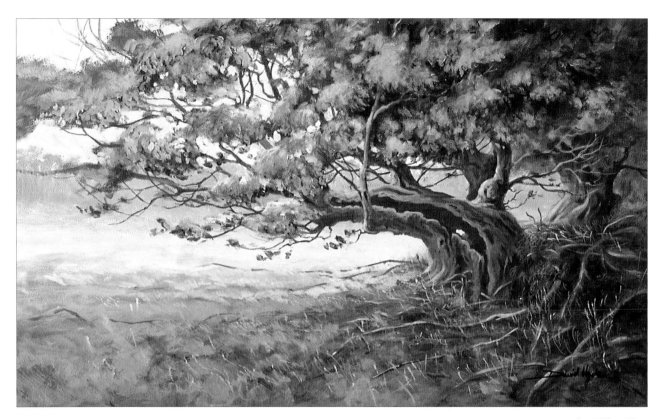

The Old Willow
43 x 25.5cm (17 x 10in)

An old willow tree dominates this painting. To evoke its size, I have let most of the tree disappear out of the top of the picture. Heavy shadow tones on the right have been balanced with the sunlight in the meadow beyond on the left. A careful balance was struck to depict the complexity of the foliage and branches without getting overly fussy.

Opposite

Field Edge – Late Summer
25 x 30.5cm (9¾ x 12in)

The soft greens have been tempered with ochre and sienna tones to give the feeling of late summer. In order to eliminate confusion, detail has been removed from the area on the right beyond the fence. This whole area has been treated with warm light tones to suggest soft Summer sunshine. A rigger brush was used for the twigs and the fence wire.

79

FLOWERS IN ACRYLICS

by Carole Massey

Flowers are an ideal subject for the artist. In the garden, from the emergence of the first snowdrops, through the glorious profusion of summer blooms to the rich, vibrant colours of autumn, there is constant inspiration. Any time of year, a wonderful array of cut flowers and pot plants is available.

Before the seventeenth century, flower painting ranked low in comparison with traditional portraiture and landscapes. But as the Dutch trade in rare flowers from the Middle East grew, exotic bulbs became a valuable commodity, and the fashionable gentry commissioned paintings of their prized specimens as proof of their wealth and social status. Today, Van Gogh's *Sunflowers* is one of the world's favourite and most widely recognised paintings.

Acrylics are a really versatile painting medium. Fast-drying, odourless, flexible and non-yellowing, they can be used on almost any prepared surface. Gels or mediums can vary their consistency from matt to glossy, from thick to thin or add texture.

The styles used in this section range from watercolour-type techniques to thick palette knife painting, and I have used methods designed to help both the newcomer to acrylics and the more experienced user to deal with the inspiring subject of flower painting. I have shown how to paint a simple pot plant using transparent washes; a rose archway in a summer garden and an oriental lily using thick brushwork and a painting knife. I shall also look at flower shapes, colour mixes, composition, tonal contrast, foliage, as well as supports and materials.

I hope this section gives you the confidence to explore the infinite variety of techniques possible with acrylic paints and opens your eyes to the simple joys of flower painting, so you will enjoy my vision and feel confident to use this exciting medium.
Happy painting!

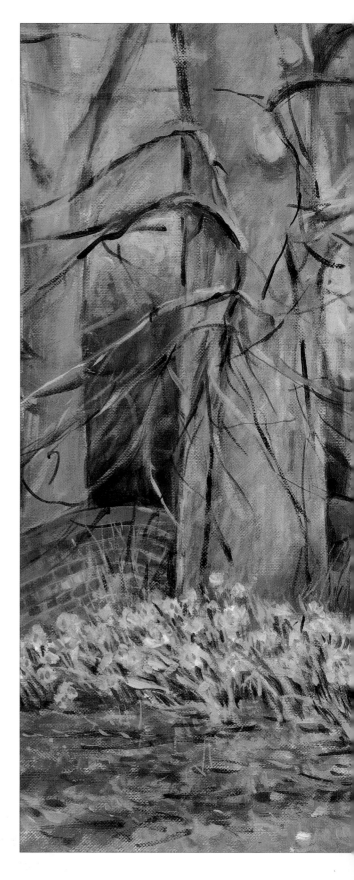

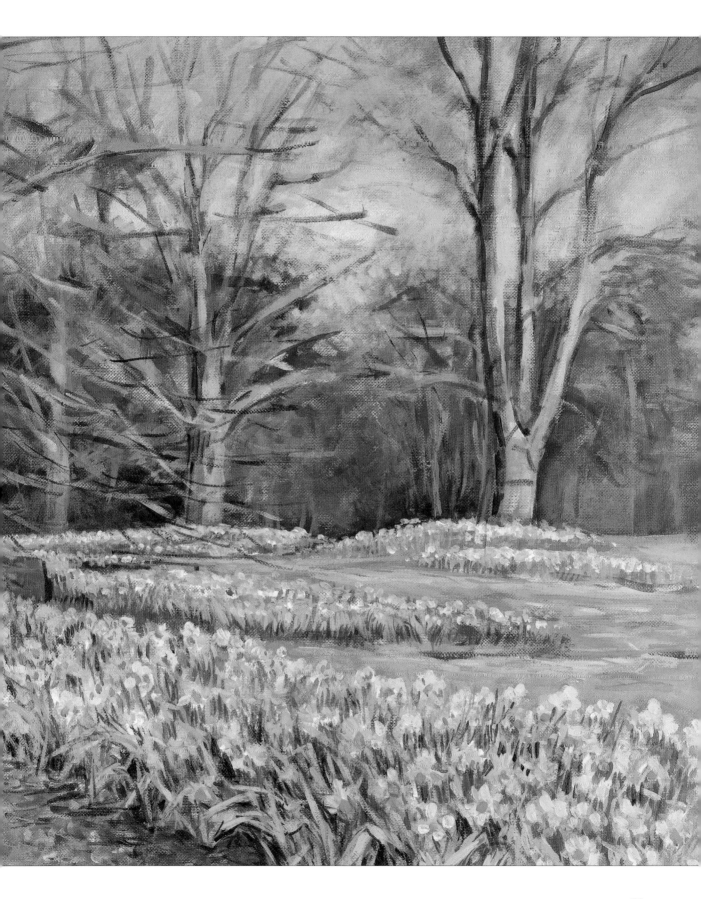

Flower colours

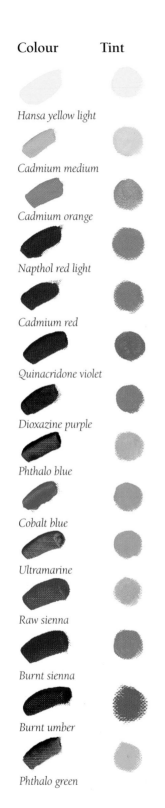

Hansa yellow light

Cadmium medium

Cadmium orange

Napthol red light

Cadmium red

Quinacridone violet

Dioxazine purple

Phthalo blue

Cobalt blue

Ultramarine

Raw sienna

Burnt sienna

Burnt umber

Phthalo green

Do not be impatient when mixing colours: it can take some time to achieve the right hue. Always try out the mixed colour before using it on your painting. If you think it might change, let it dry thoroughly to estimate colour shift.

The **primary colours** yellow, red and blue cannot be made from any other colours. **Secondary colours** are made by mixing two primaries: orange (yellow plus red); green (yellow plus blue); and purple (red plus blue). To reproduce the flamboyant, clear colours of nature, it is often best to use ready-mixed single pigment secondary colours like cadmium orange, dioxazine purple or phthalo green. They are far brighter than colours mixed using two primaries, and the effect will be much more vibrant – see page 116 *Orange on Blue*. **Complementary colours** are pairs of colours that sit opposite one another on a colour wheel and balance and enhance one another: blue and orange; red and green; yellow and purple. Blue can be enlivened by placing orange next to it. Be aware of the merit of complementary colours, particularly when mixing shadows: instead of using black or brown to darken, add the complementary colour to create more interesting effects. Mix a touch of purple into the shadow on a yellow daffodil petal, or naturalise an area suffused with green by adding a little red or brown.

Opacity and transparency

Information on whether colours are transparent (TP), translucent (TL) or opaque (O) will be given on the label of most good-quality paints. Transparent colours allow colour underneath to show through and are ideal for glazing. Translucent colours allow some light to pass through. Opaque colours reflect light, give the best coverage, and therefore make most impact. White is used to lighten colours or create tints: I buy large tubes as I use more of it than any other colour. Titanium white is bright, opaque, and ideal for highlights, while zinc or mixing white is softer, transparent and ideal for tints – see left.

Warm and cool colours

Knowing when to use warm or cool colours will produce more effective results. Cool lemon yellow plus a greenish blue such as phthalo blue will make a bright spring green, while cadmium yellow, which is warm, plus a reddish blue such as ultramarine will make warm olive green. A cool red such as quinacridone violet mixed with cobalt blue will make a beautiful purple, whereas a warm red such as cadmium red used with the same blue will produce a far greyer or browner result.

Colour shift

This effect occurs because the acrylic/water emulsion is milky when wet and may appear slightly lighter. As the water evaporates the binder becomes clear and the colour can darken slightly. The effect is less pronounced with modern acrylics.

Flower colour wheel

This 'colour wheel' shows some of the most useful mixes.

Red (nasturtium)
*cadmium red medium and
cadmium orange*

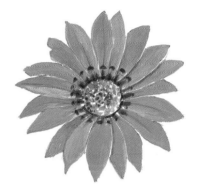

Orange (gazania)
*cadmium orange and napthol red light;
burnt umber and red markings*

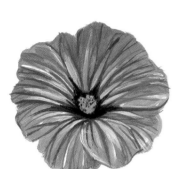

Bluish red (lavatera)
quinacridone violet and white

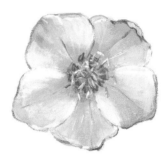

White (hellebore)
*white with a touch of phthalo
green plus quinacridone violet*

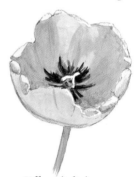

Yellow (tulip)
*cadmium yellow with a touch of
cadmium red medium; a touch of purple
in the shadows*

Purple and lilac (polyanthus)
purple, ultramarine and white

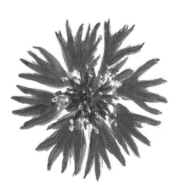

Warm blue (cornflower)
cobalt and white

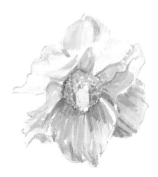

Green-blue (Himalayan poppy)
phthalo blue and white

83

Mixing greens

Practise mixing different greens to add depth and interest. In general, bluer cooler colours recede and warmer colours come forward in a painting. Hansa yellow or cadmium yellow light will produce a cooler, more acid green, whereas cadmium yellow medium will make a warmer olive green. A small amount of red or burnt sienna added to a bright green will neutralise it. Try mixing some of these examples to give you an idea of the wide variety of hues that can be achieved.

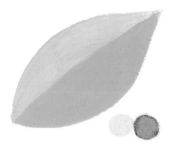

Phthalo green and hansa yellow

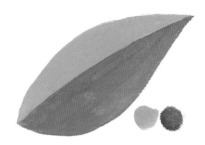

Permanent green light and ultramarine

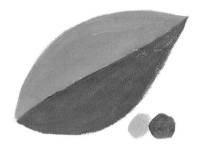

Cobalt blue, cadmium yellow and white

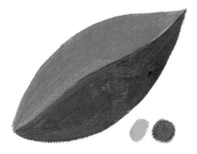

Cadmium yellow and ultramarine

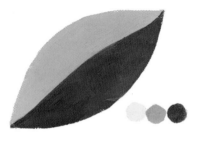

Phthalo green, lemon yellow, dioxazine purple and white

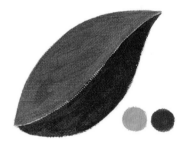

Permanent green and cadmium red

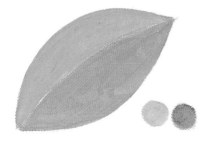

Cadmium yellow and phthalo green

Tip

Try to paint in this sequence: bright – dark – light. Paint the general colours and tones first, then the darkest areas. Put in the lightest colours and highlights last.

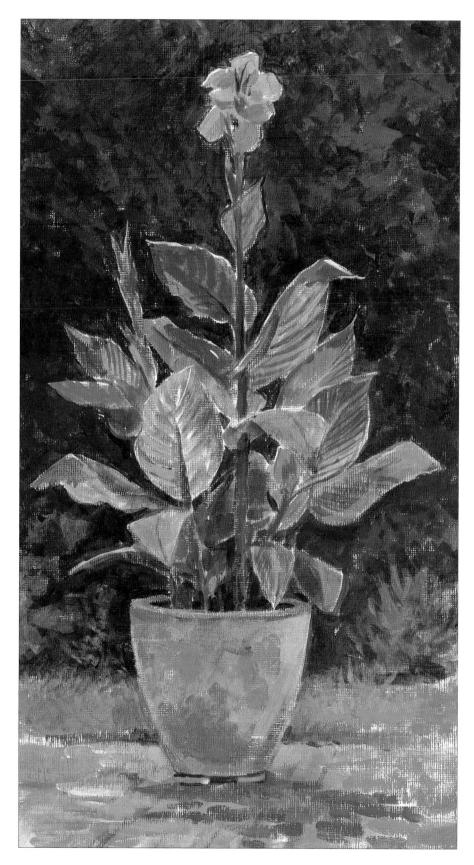

Canna Lily in Sunlight
20 x 36cm (8 x 14in)

*It was a very hot day when I painted
this, so I had to work rapidly as even
with a retarder added to my paint,
it was still drying fast. I captured
the glowing orange, red and green
striped foliage first and then added
a patchwork of brush strokes using
purple, phthalo green and burnt
sienna to create a strong dark
background in contrast.*

Flower shapes & drawing

Though there is an emphasis on painting in this book, I cannot
overestimate the importance of drawing. Accurate observation, sketching
the plant growth, and understanding its shape and form, will greatly
improve a finished painting. Always try to draw what you see, not what
you *think* you see. As with any other form of drawing, be sure to look at
the proportions, comparing the height to the width of the flower or plant,
and observing the negative shapes – those spaces between the flowers and
foliage or between one petal and the next – which will help you to draw the
rest more precisely.

Begin your study by sketching lightly with a B or 2B pencil. When you
are happy with your drawing, go over it using a neutral colour that will
blend in with the colours in the painting. I usually use raw sienna, burnt
sienna or cobalt blue. As you redraw, do not merely outline your pencil
drawing but keep observing the subject, altering and improving, making
each stage exploratory.

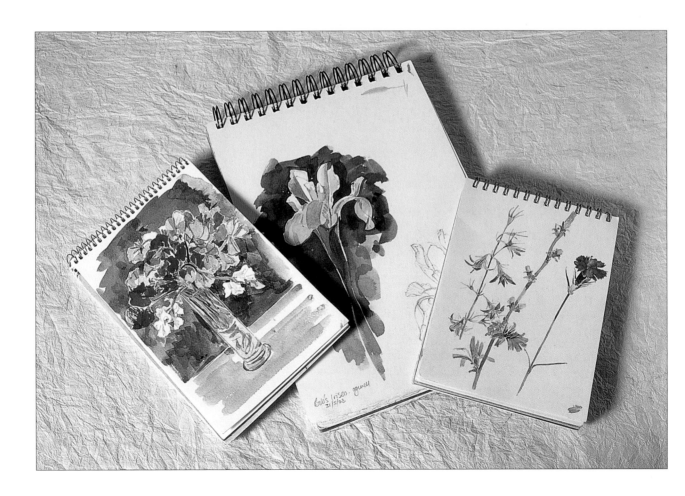

Round

Simplify these chrysanthemum heads by thinking of them as a series of discs, turning towards and away from the viewer. The pattern and centre of these flowers form a series of concentric circles – which when viewed from an angle make up a series of ellipses. The flower head is not flat but dips in the centre, so observe carefully how the ellipses change in shape.

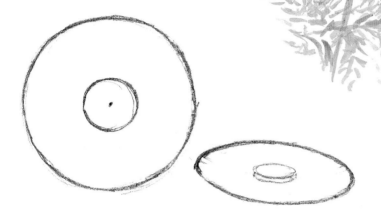

Trumpets

For a trumpet-shaped flower like these daffodils, lightly draw a circle or ellipse and in the centre, a cylinder, flared at the open end. Six equally spaced points on the circle mark where the tips of the petals touch it. Details like the frill at the trumpet mouth and the ribs in the petals can be added afterwards.

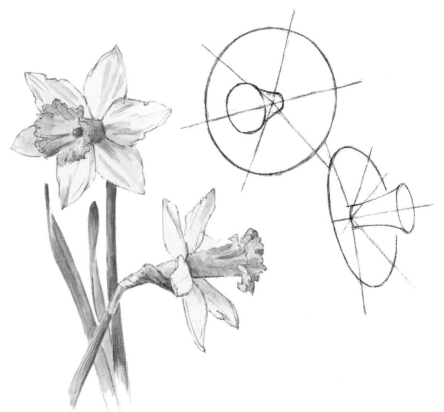

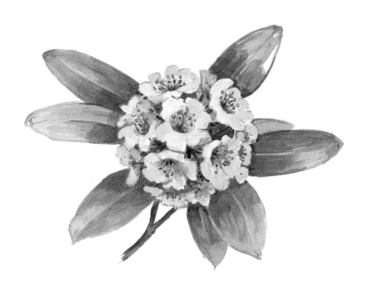

Multi-headed

In this example of a rhododendron, the overall shape is spherical but the flower head is made up of lots of smaller round flowers. Treat it as a group of individual round shapes, noting how the ellipses become shallower as they move over the sphere.

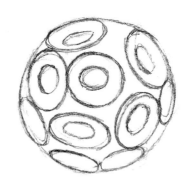

Bells

For each individual flower on this Canterbury bell, lightly draw an angled T shape and construct the bell shape round it, with two equal halves either side of the vertical line, and an ellipse across the bar of the T. Turning your drawing upside down can help you to construct equal halves.

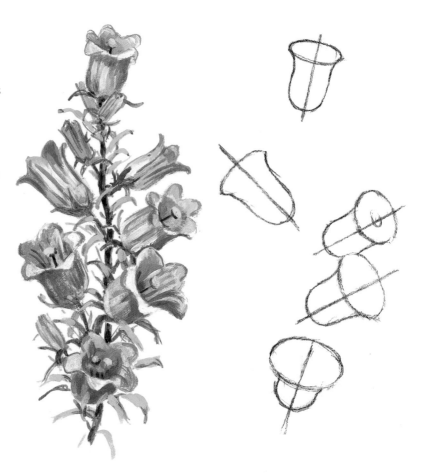

Spikes

Flowers like these delphiniums are made up of a series of smaller flowers, positioned round a cylindrical shape that comes to a point at the top.

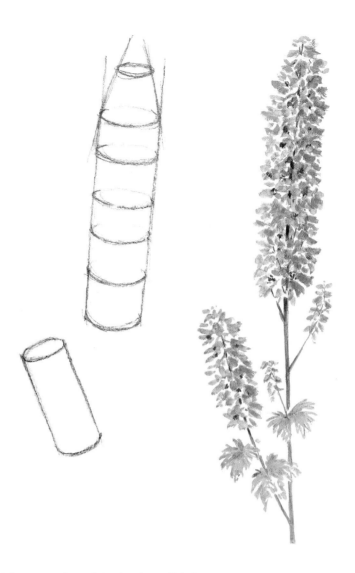

Stars

For a star-shaped flower such as this nicotiana, lightly draw four, five or six lines radiating from the centre of a circle or ellipse to points on the rim, to establish the centre of each petal.

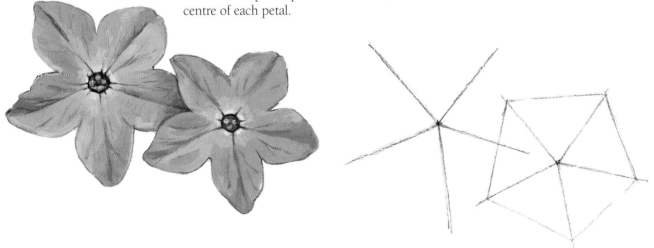

Composition for flowers

Start by making a small, simple thumbnail sketch so you can see whether the layout and tones look right. Try to avoid a strong vertical or horizontal emphasis in the centre of your composition, placing it instead about a third of the way into the picture plane – the 'rule of thirds'. Where these lines divide are the focal points, which are the ideal places to place an accent – see the large tree in *Daffodils in the Park*, page 80–81 or the fountain in *Hollyhocks Against the Wall*, page 111. A repeated motif is often interesting – see pages 92 and 93. Group warm and cool colours to help balance the composition.

When you have worked out the composition, enlarge it to fit your paper or canvas. Look at the *negative* shapes – the spaces between the flowers – to aid accuracy. If you are painting outdoors, look at the light source. If you intend to work for any length of time, how quickly will the shadows change and alter your chosen scene? Sometimes it is best to paint for a limited period, at the same time, for several days running. You can set up two or three paintings this way.

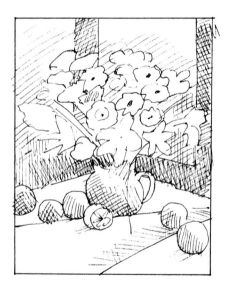

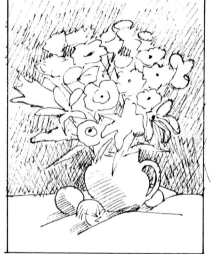

Imperfect composition

* *The jug has been placed centrally.*

* *The shape of the white cloth seems to merge awkwardly with the jug's neck.*

* *In the background, a strong vertical hangs off the edge of the composition.*

* *The eye is led out of the picture by strong diagonals in the folds of cloth and the fruit at the painting's edges.*

Better composition

* *The slightly off-centre jug makes the composition more interesting.*

* *The simplified background enhances the composition.*

* *The fruit by the jug helps to ensure that the flowers are the focal point.*

* *The plainer background helps to emphasise the jug's shape.*

Tip

You may find a viewfinder useful to help to decide how much to include in a painting, and its format.

Opposite
Bouquet in Blue Jug
27 x 35cm (10½ x 14in)

I had always wanted to use this blue jug in a painting and the colours of a lovely bouquet I was given complemented it perfectly. I used a multi-coloured cloth to echo the blue, orange and yellow in the arrangement and began by dotting in the relative positions of the flower centres and drawing in the jug lightly. I had decided to alter the background to suit my composition – see the sketches opposite – but was not happy with my first choice of a neutral mix of raw and burnt sienna and white. I left it on my easel for several weeks waiting for inspiration, then a painter friend visited and suggested that I should try reds. Hey presto, it worked – thanks Sue!

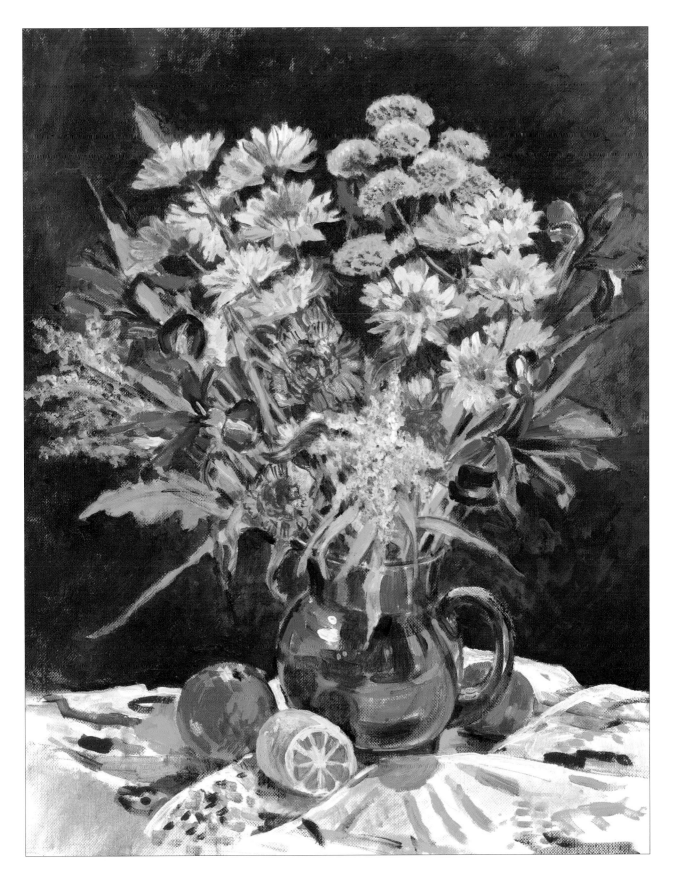

91

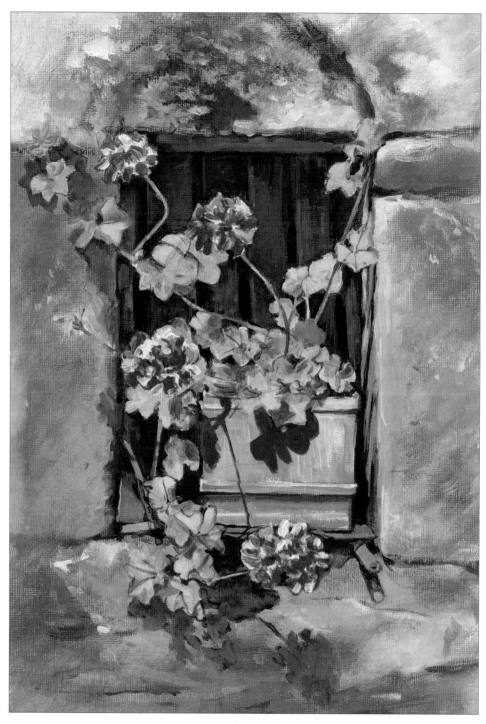

Pink Geraniums in Niche
25 x 36cm (10 x 14in)

The wow factor! What made this a stunning subject for me was the pink of the geraniums leaping out of the dark recess. But there are other bonuses – the colour of the flowers is repeated in the container, and the shape of the container is echoed in the rectangular shape of the niche, outlined by the softer handling and colours of the surrounding wall. I used scumbling, dry brush and splattering effects to achieve the rough texture of the stonework.

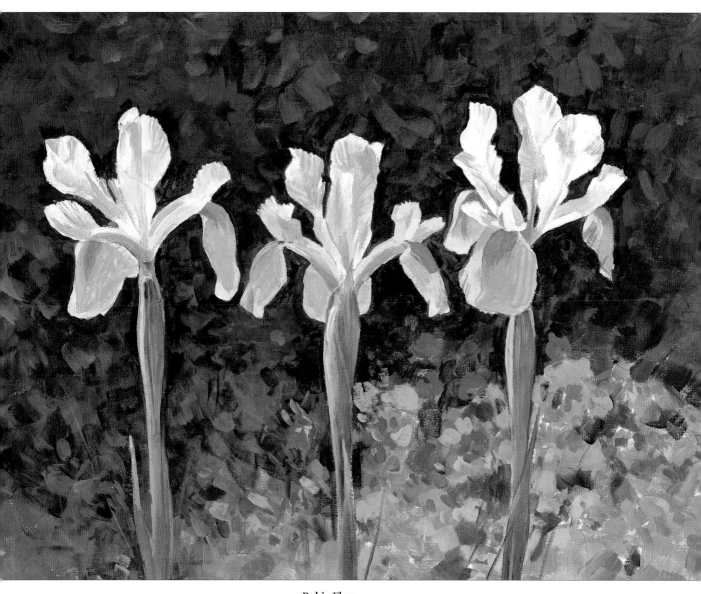

Bob's Flags
51 x 38cm (20 x 15in)

Three identical blooms, poised like ballet dancers waiting to perform, set against a rich backdrop of dark greens and blues. Although they look unreal, this is just as I painted these flag irises in a friend's garden. I used high key colours – pale yellows, and delicate pale grey/blue shadows to emphasise the brilliance of light filtering through semi-transparent petals, which contrasted with the cool pink, lilacs and bluish greens of a mound of geraniums below.

Tone

Tone means how light or dark something is. When I am asked to explain why a painting is not working, the most usual answer is lack of tonal contrast, which is more important than colour to make a painting come to life. Sketching a subject first in pencil can help to establish the tonal values before you start to paint. If you half-close your eyes before you look at your subject matter it will make it easier to assess the tones. Note that dark foliage can often be deceptively light in tone if it has a reflective surface.

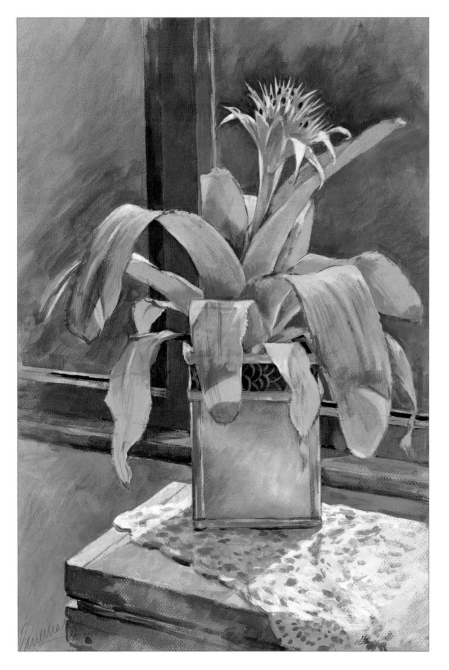

Cactus With Pink Flower
35 x 52cm (14 x 20½in)

I used grey textured paper and worked with matt acrylic paint enabling me to create a pastel-like effect in this staged still life. The reflected highlights and pools of fragmented sunlight through the leaves are in sharp contrast to the cast shadows and darker background tones.

Opposite
Hemerocalis and Ivy
28 x 38cm (11 x 15in)

This hot, vibrant flower portrait is one in which sorting out the contrasting tones and colours was crucial to making this busy subject work. The alternating cool greens of the Hemerocalis leaves and the warm greens of the variegated ivy interweave across the painting surface.

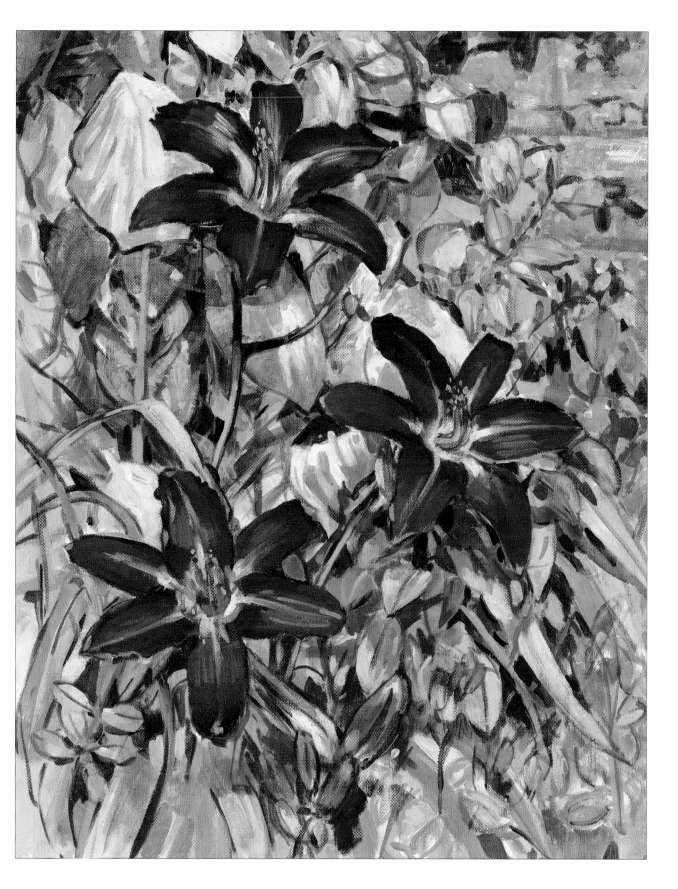

Techniques for flowers

Acrylics can be used in many different ways, according to the effect you want to achieve. They can be used conventionally with a brush, or more thickly in an 'impasto' style with a painting knife. They can also be thinned and used like watercolour, though as each transparent layer dries it becomes permanent, and will not 'lift' or mix in and become muddied by successive layers. Their normal drying time is between five and fifteen minutes, but thick layers may take longer. Extremely thick layers may take several days, but are still much faster drying than oils. These examples show a range of the techniques I use.

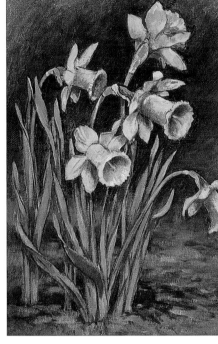

Perspective
First Daffodils

The trumpeting daffodil heralds the warmer seasons to come, but capturing their distinctive shapes can be a challenge. Their vibrant yellow heads seem to twist and turn against the backdrop of dull, bare earth. I used complementary colours – purples and blues – for the shadows in the trumpets and petals to make them look three-dimensional. Mix purple in with the browns to achieve consistency throughout the painting.

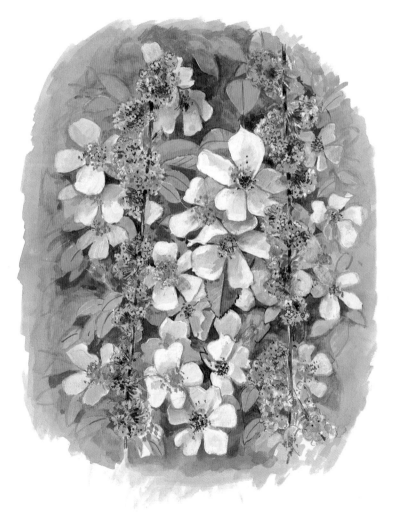

Glazing
Single Roses and Buddleia

I added blending medium to extend the colour without affecting its intensity, and built up thin, transparent layers of paint to achieve a subtle glow. I painted successive layers of greens in the foliage, working from light to dark. To lighten a colour when glazing, add more water and medium: never use white, which is opaque.

Thin to thick
Orange Tiger Lily

I drew the lily and complex leaves, observing the negative spaces. I started painting thin washes of colour for the background, flowers and leaves, gradually increasing the thickness of the paint on the plant: ultramarine, hansa yellow and white for the leaves, and cadmium orange and cadmium yellow on the bright flowers, where the paint was thickest, to make them stand out.

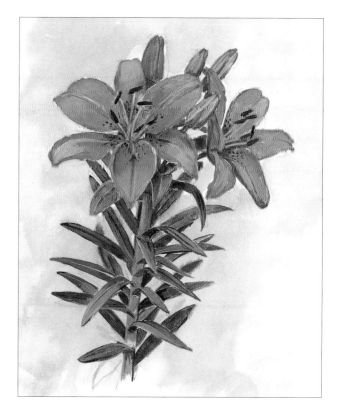

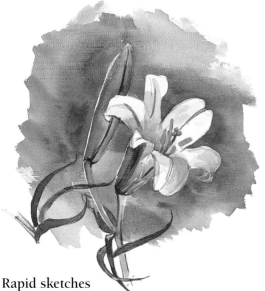

Rapid sketches
White Lily

For this study on acrylic/oil paper I used a watercolour technique that is useful for producing quick outdoor studies of growing plants. A few patches of undiluted pigment in the background suggest a backdrop of blue flowers that could be developed further.

Christmas Cactus and Wooden Mannequin

I used only a 6mm (¼in) flat bristle brush for this loose and swiftly painted subject on rough watercolour paper, to take advantage of some fleeting winter sunshine streaming on to the window sill.

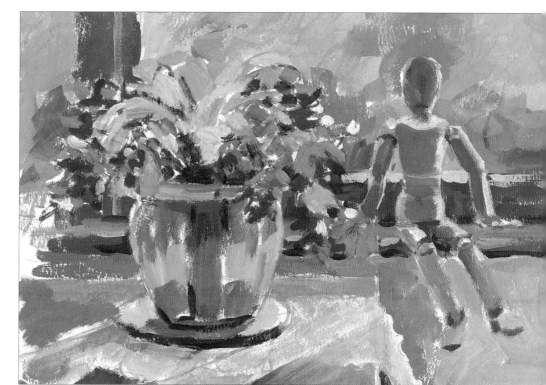

Primulas

Simple studies of flowers can be amazingly effective, but you do not need to spend a lot of money on expensive blooms. These little plants cost just pennies, and when you have finished painting you can put them in the garden. I used the plant as a starting point for my drawing, but changed details like the position of individual flowers and leaves to improve the composition. The final touch was the suggestion of a plant pot, replacing the uninspiring shiny plastic of the original pot with a more aesthetically pleasing hint of terracotta.

This was a quick, spontaneous study. The paint was used like watercolour, allowing the white of the paper to shine through thin applications of colour. The colours were mixed with water with a few drops of flow enhancer added to encourage the paint to mix better.

You will need

140lb (300gsm) semi-rough (Not) watercolour paper, 25 x 30cm (10 x 12in)

Flow enhancer

2B pencil

Putty eraser

Brushes: No. 1 and No. 4 round

Paints: cadmium yellow light; cadmium yellow medium; cadmium red; raw sienna; ultramarine; phthalo blue; dioxazine purple; titanium white

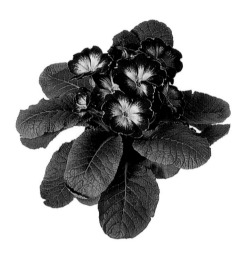

The small potted plant.

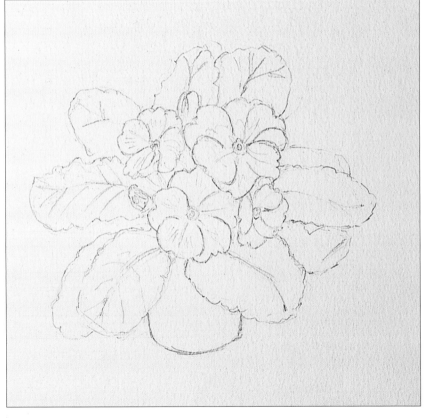

1. Using a 2B pencil, establish the main outlines of the plant.

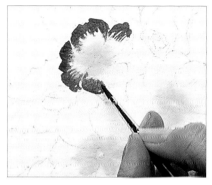

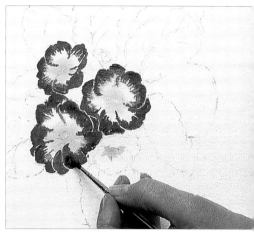

2. Using the No. 1 round brush and cadmium yellow light, put in the yellow markings in the flower centres, wetting the outer edges with water to encourage the colour to run slightly.

3. Using the same brush and purple with a little ultramarine, put in the edges of the flowers, dampening the paper with water towards the middle of the flower to lighten the colour.

4. Using a slightly thicker mix of the same colour, darken the edge of the petals, leaving a tiny space of white paper between the flowers and wetting round the yellow where necessary.

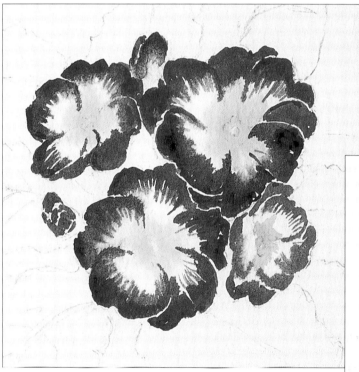

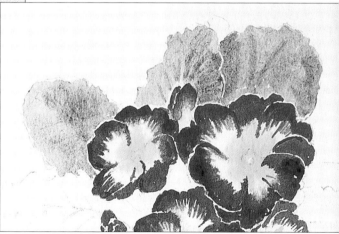

5. When you are satisfied with the way you have built up the purple tones, leave your work to dry.

6. Using the larger brush, paint a mix of ultramarine and cadmium yellow light into the leaves. Add a little more ultramarine and work over them wet into wet with this darker mix so the colours blend slightly.

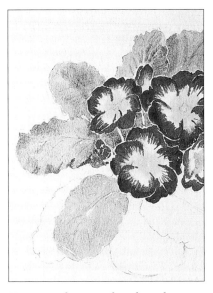

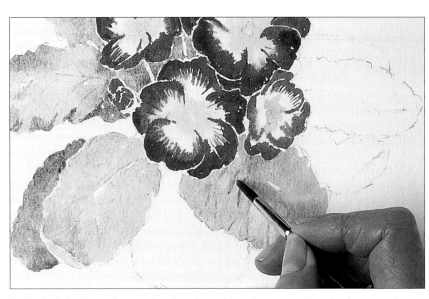

7. Using the same brush and a phthalo blue and cadmium yellow light mix, put a light wash of colour on the lower leaves.

8. Switch back to the smaller brush and continue to paint the leaves using a range of tones and colours.

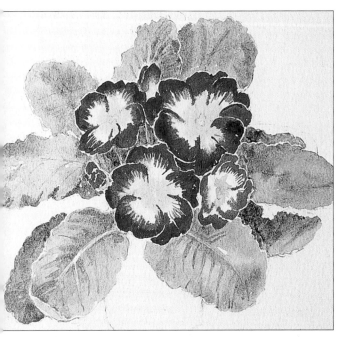

9. Paint in the veins on some of the leaves...

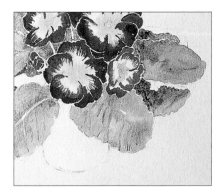

10. ... varying the amount of detail so that they do not all look the same.

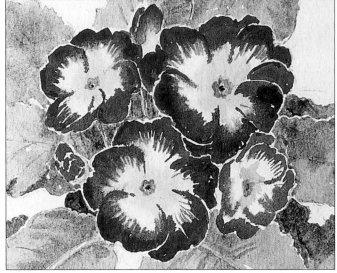

11. Using the small round brush and a mix of ultramarine and cadmium yellow medium, put in the darker flower centres.

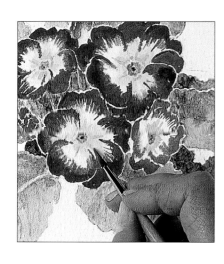

12. Using the small brush and raw sienna, add fine lines to the yellow markings in the centres.

13. Using the larger brush and a thin mix of cadmium yellow medium, cadmium red and a touch of purple, paint in the pot. While it is still wet, take some purple wash on the brush tip and touch it into the surface wet in wet to create shading.

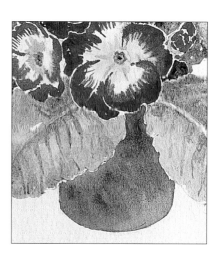

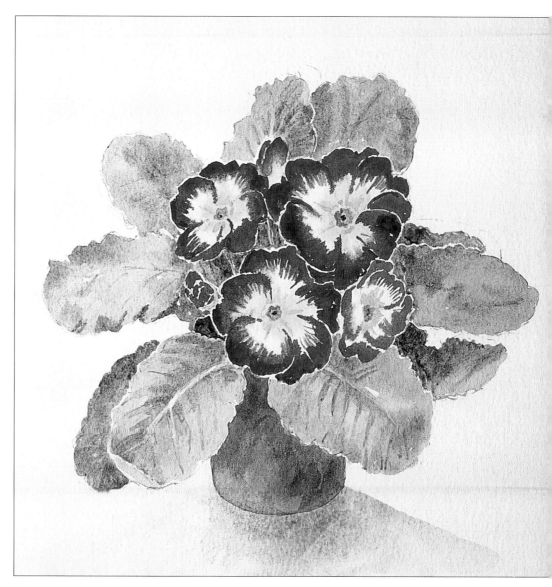

The finished picture

I added the shadows under the pot using a thin mix of ultramarine and purple and re-established highlights using titanium white.

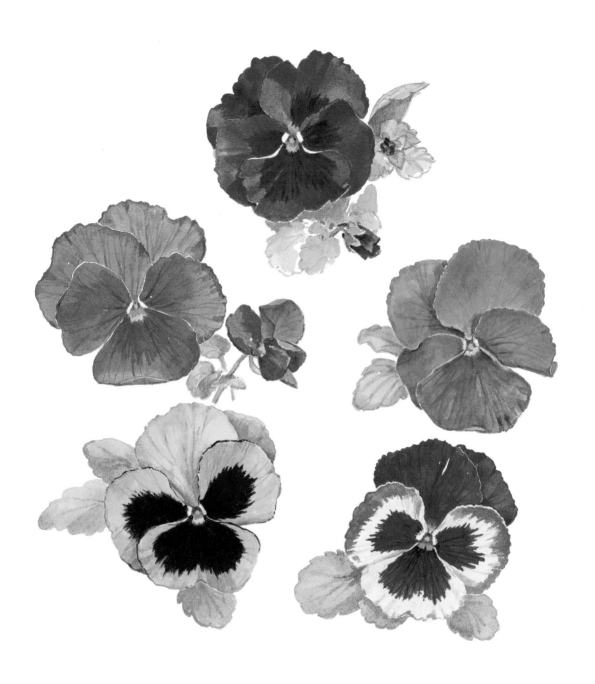

Five Pansies

Pansies are always delightful to paint, and are well suited to watercolour-type techniques. Each flower can be painted separately and – if necessary – on different occasions to produce a more formal composition. I used a wet in wet technique on HP watercolour paper and added a flow enhancer to encourage the paint to mix more freely. The darker markings in the centre of the petals were painted, then while they were still wet, they were encouraged to run by dampening the adjacent paper with a slightly wetted brush.

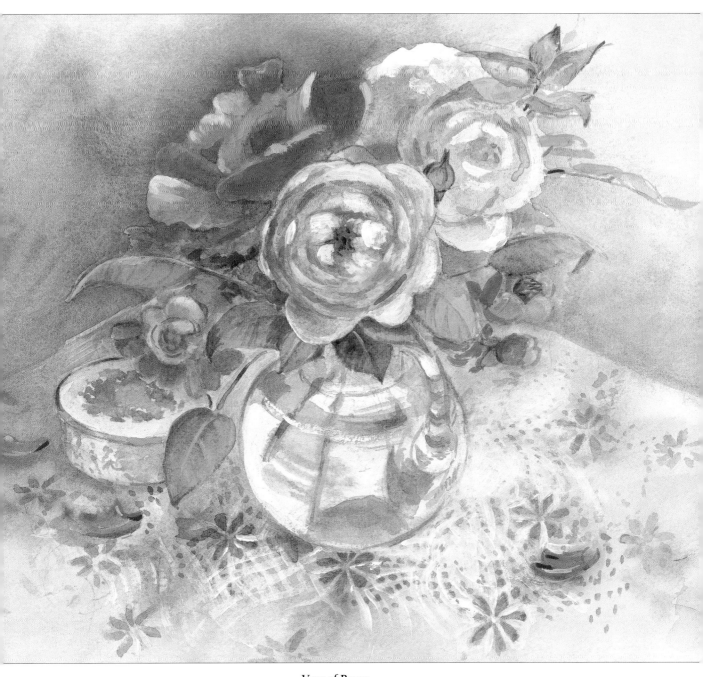

Vase of Roses

48 x 33cm (19 x 13in)

This painting, in which I have used the acrylic paints just like watercolour, demonstrates the versatility of the medium. The advantage of acrylic over watercolour is that when they are dry, the washes do not lift or mix and become dull. Some of the light areas, especially in the vase, were achieved by reserving the white of the watercolour paper, but in other areas, such as the tablecloth, I added titanium white to emphasise the pattern.

Rose Arch

Though drawing or painting from life is the ideal, it is not always possible. Photographs, particularly those you have taken yourself, are a good alternative. Do not try to copy them slavishly, as the photographic process can distort the true colours of nature: the sky may be bleached out, or shadows may appear unnaturally dark brown or black. Remember that you can move elements around to make a better composition – see page 90 – or simplify them, as I have done here. The dappled shadows across the path are very important: they increase the tonal contrast and really make the painting sparkle.

You will need

Canvas board 30.5 x 40.5cm (12 x 16in)

2B pencil

Putty eraser

Brushes: No 1, No. 4 and No. 8 round; No. 1 flat; No. 2 rigger

Paints: cadmium yellow light; cadmium yellow; cadmium red; quinacridone violet; cobalt blue; ultramarine; phthalo green; dioxazine purple; raw sienna; burnt sienna; titanium white

Gloss medium

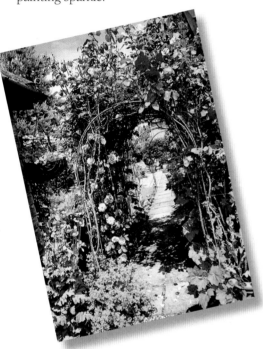

The paint mixes I used:

Roses: quinacridone violet and white

Wall: cadmium yellow, raw sienna, burnt sienna and white

Path: cadmium yellow, raw sienna and white

Foliage: phthalo green and white; phthalo green and cadmium yellow light

Darker foliage: ultramarine and cadmium yellow

Very dark foliage: phthalo green and dioxazine purple

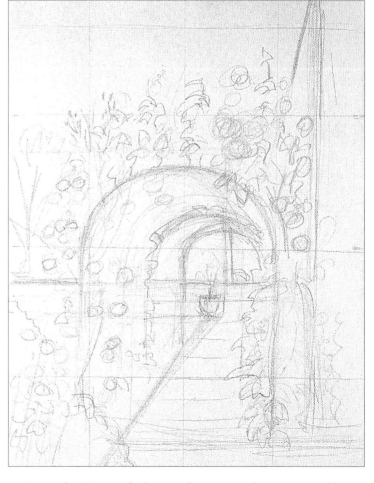

1. Using the 2B pencil, draw in the main outlines. Use grid lines to help position the main elements onto the canvas board.

2. Mix all the main washes and with the No. 1 brush, put in the first suggestion of colour as a placement guide.

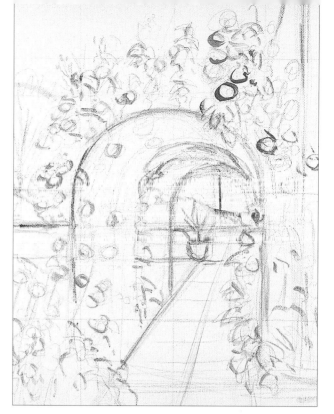

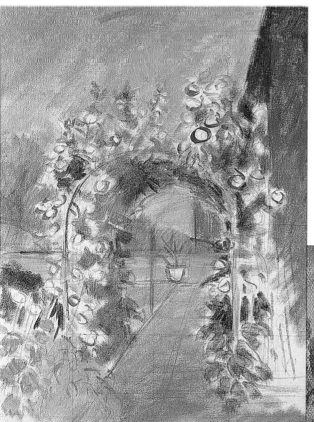

3. Using the No. 8 brush, begin to block in all the main areas of colour.

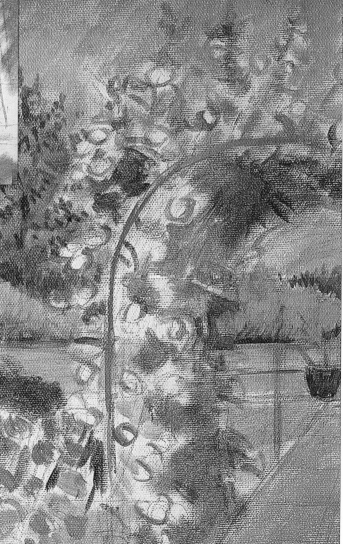

4. Build up further tones, adding the mauve flowers and some darker detail to the tree in the top corner. Paint in the pot using cobalt blue.

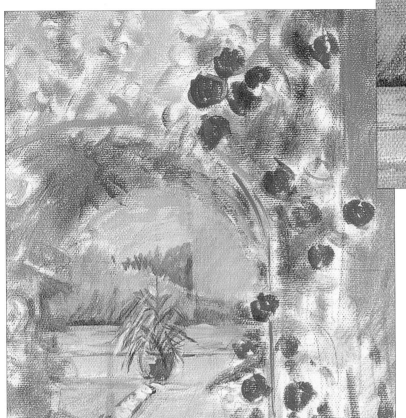

5. Work on the foliage, adding touches of darker green leaves. Put in the shapes of the red flowers roughly using cadmium red. Paint in the plant, then add highlights to the pot using a mix of cobalt blue and titanium white.

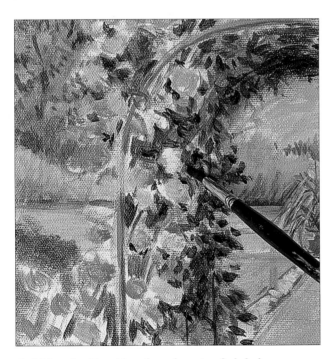

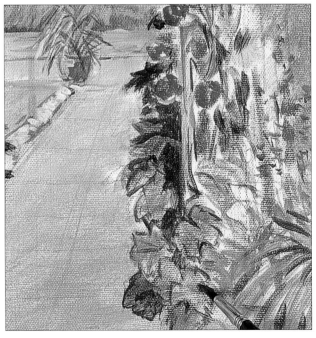

6. Using the No. 4 brush and a mix of phthalo green and dioxazine purple, put in the dark green tones of the foliage round the roses.

7. Using the same deep green mix and brush, go into the lower right section of the painting and paint round the outlines of the leaves.

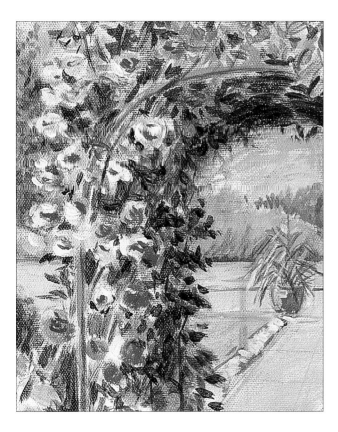

8. Using the same brush, lighten the roses with a mix of quinacridone violet and titanium white.

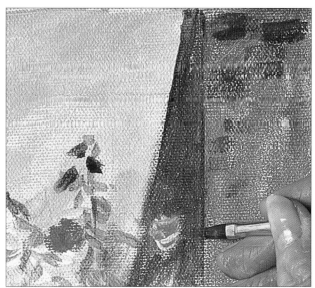

9. Using the No. 1 flat brush, add brickwork details to the wall using a mix of raw sienna and burnt sienna, adding some purple for the shaded side.

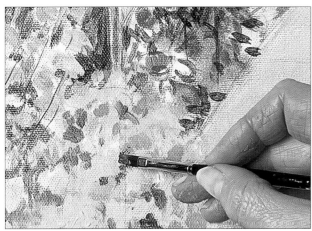

10. Mix white, cadmium yellow light and a touch of phthalo green and use the same brush to add the clump of light foliage at the front.

11. Add details of the second pair of arches with the dark green mix and the No. 2 rigger. Add spots of white for the flowers in the border.

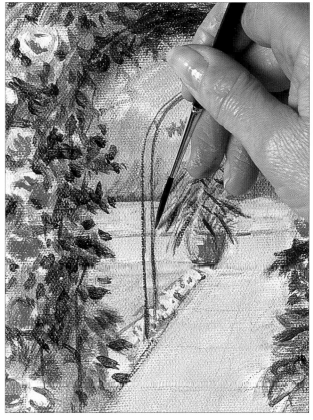

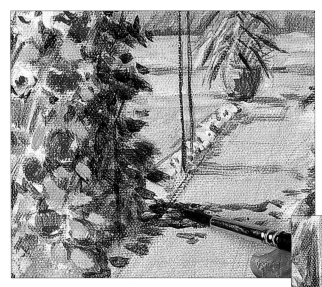

12. Using a No. 4 brush and a mix of raw sienna and dioxazine purple, paint the dappled shadow across the path.

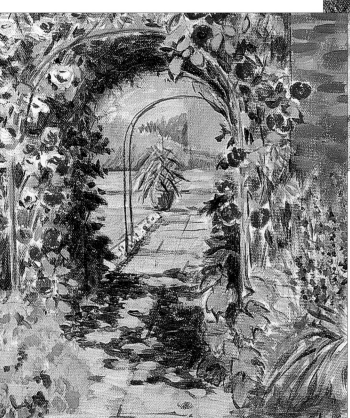

13. Using the same brush and shadow mix, paint in the lines of paving in perspective.

14. Using a mix of cadmium yellow light, raw sienna and titanium white, lighten areas of the path, going over some of the shadow if necessary. Using a mix of ultramarine and white, paint the delphiniums on the right.

Opposite
The finished painting
I applied a thin glaze of burnt sienna over the right hand area of wall and the path at the lower edge of the canvas to make the colour warmer, thus creating a greater sense of depth. Using the dioxazine purple and phthalo green mix, I added more shadow detail to the foreground foliage by picking out the negative spaces. Notice how the greatest amount of detail is reserved for the plants that are nearest. Finally I added any really bright highlights that were needed on the roses, the centres to the lilac poppies, the arch and the path to complete the painting.

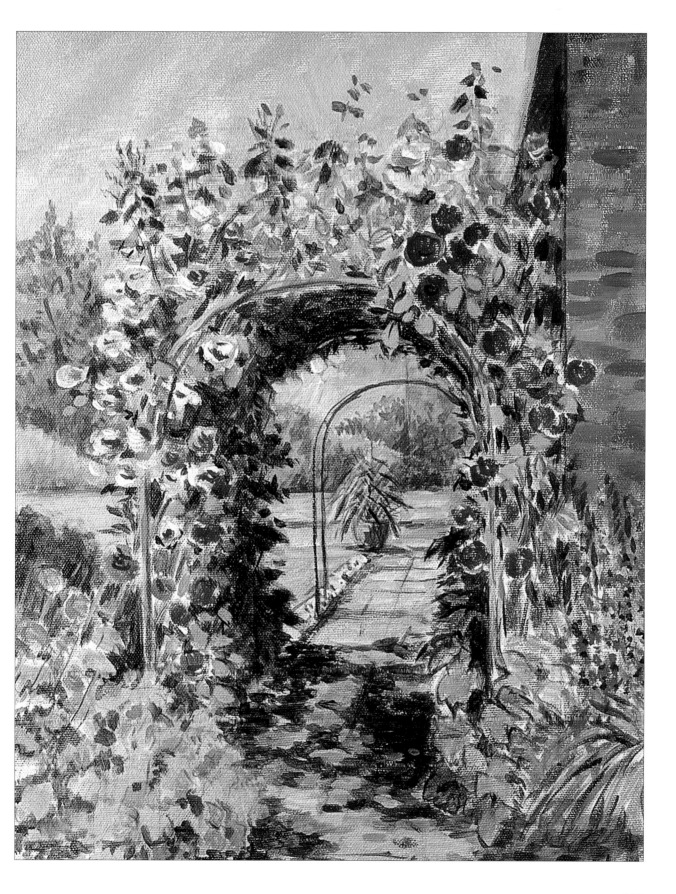

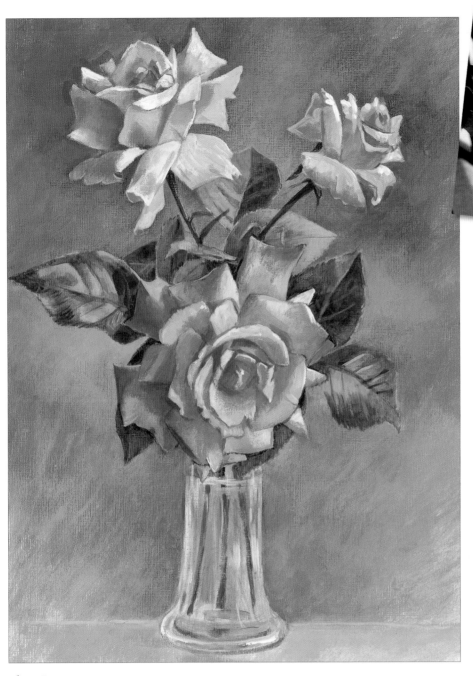

The photograph
I worked from.

Three Roses
27 x 38cm (10½ x 15in)

All too often, I see something that would make a wonderful painting but have no time to sit down and paint it. Photographs are the only option, but often the subtlety of the colours is lost and the backgrounds become dark and flat, so they need enhancing. I brought these wonderful, full-blown roses back to life on white linen-finish acrylic paper, by enhancing the pinks and yellows. I used warm blues and greys to make the background interesting and to contrast with the flowers.

Opposite
**Hollyhocks
Against the Wall**
24 x 37cm (9½ x 14½ in)

The perspective of the wall, paving slabs and hollyhocks leads the eye to the focal point of the painting, the fountain. The tone of the hollyhock stems and buds is dependent on whether they are set against a dark or a light background.

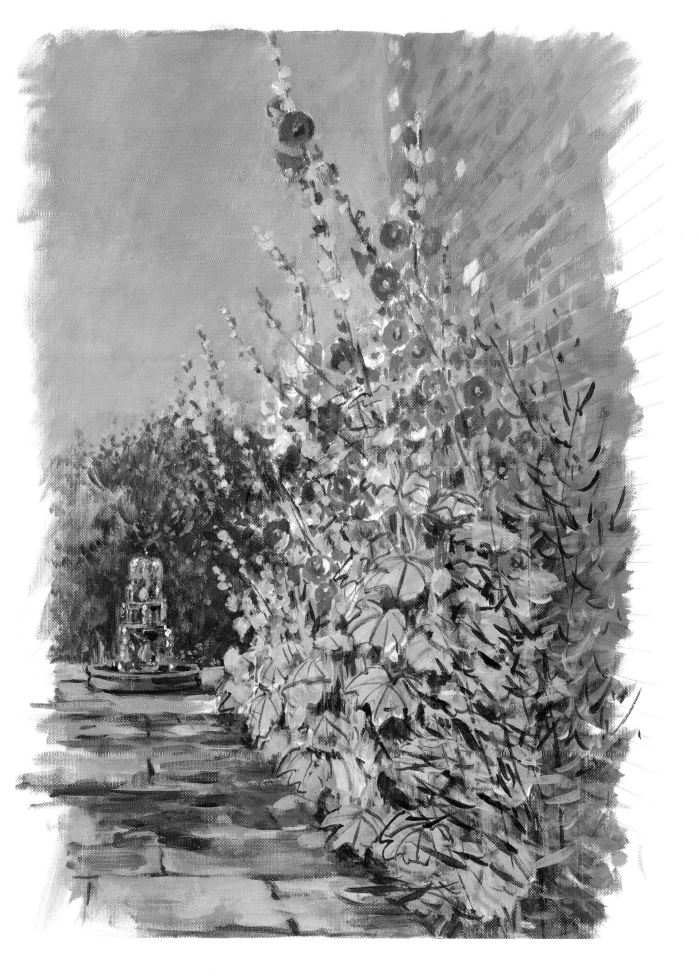

Stargazer Lilies

Stargazer lilies are a delightful subject. I took a single stem to study and stained the whole surface of the paper before starting to paint. To capture the vibrancy of the flowers, I blocked in the basic tones first, then built up the intense tones by adding layers of colour. I used blending medium with water to mix the colours, and added gels in the final stages of the painting to make the stamens and markings on the petals three dimensional. I used gloss gel as a blending medium rather than water to lighten the colours, as it keeps the colour transparent and allows the drawing to show through. The background behind the flowers was darkened to increase tonal contrast.

You will need

Textured acrylic paper
43 x 53cm (17 x 21in) stretched on a board

2B pencil

Brushes: range of rounds and filberts including a No. 8 bristle filbert and a No. 1 rigger

Paints: cadmium yellow; raw sienna; quinacridone violet; burnt sienna; phthalo blue; cobalt blue; dioxazine purple; burnt umber; titanium white

Mediums: gloss medium; heavy gloss gel; thick gel

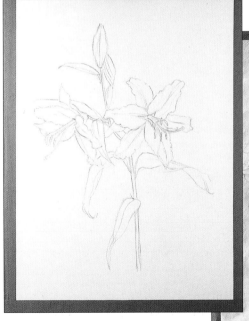

1. Using a 2B pencil, take time to make an accurate drawing.

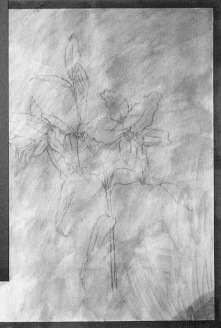

2. Using the No. 8 filbert and a mix of raw sienna, burnt sienna and blending medium, stain the surface with a thin wash that allows the drawing to show through.

112

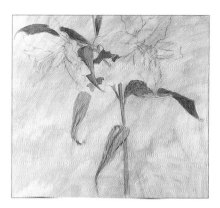

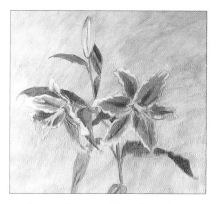

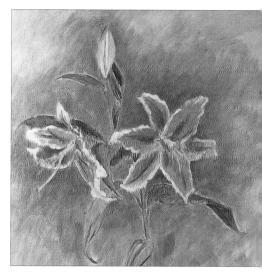

3. Using the Nos. 6 and 8 round brushes and a mix of cobalt blue and cadmium yellow, begin to block in the leaves and stems. Add a touch of phthalo blue to the mix for the darker tones.

4. Using the No. 8 brush and a mix of quinacridone violet and white, paint the pink flowers. Use a deeper mix of the same colours in the centre and paint the frilly edge white.

5. Using the staining mix with a touch more burnt sienna added, plus a little dioxazine purple, and a large brush, darken the background behind the flowers.

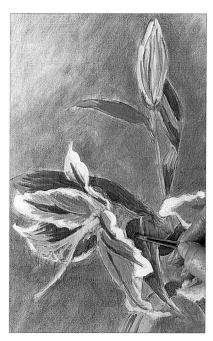

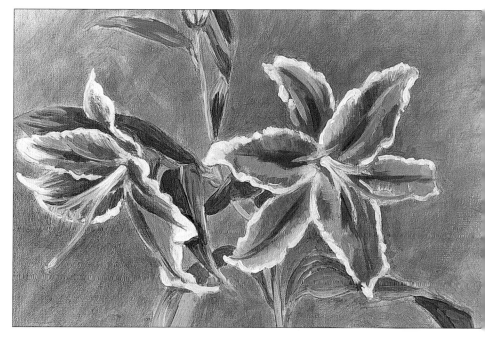

6. The buds contain hints of pale green and pale pink. Darken the leaves behind the flowers to make them stand out even more using the same mix as in step 3.

7. Using the Nos. 6 and 8 brushes, carry on adding more detail and depth to the flowers. Darken the pink with blue or purple for shading.

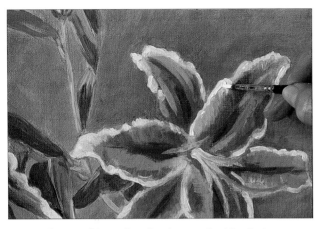

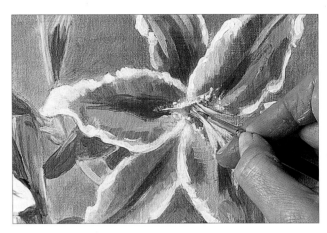

8. Mix heavy gloss gel with white and a No. 1 rigger, put in the edges of the petals.

9. Using the same brush and a mix of cobalt blue and cadmium yellow, start to work on the flower centre and the filaments of the stamen.

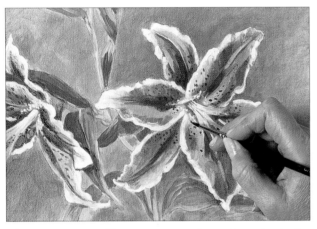

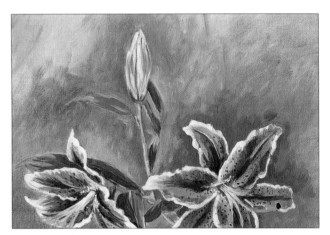

10. Using a mix of burnt sienna and purple, paint in the characteristic spots on the petals.

11. Using a large brush, glaze the background with a thin wash of burnt sienna, purple and blending medium. Let some of the brush marks show.

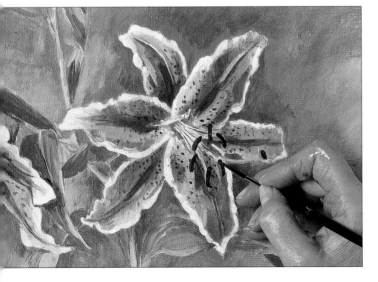

12. Using a mix of burnt umber and cadmium yellow with thick gel added, paint the brown anthers on the tips of the stamens. This will make them stand out from the surface of the painting.

Opposite
The finished picture
I added white highlights to the leaves and stamens and adjusted the background, darkening behind the light areas and lightening where necessary behind dark leaves and parts of the flowers.

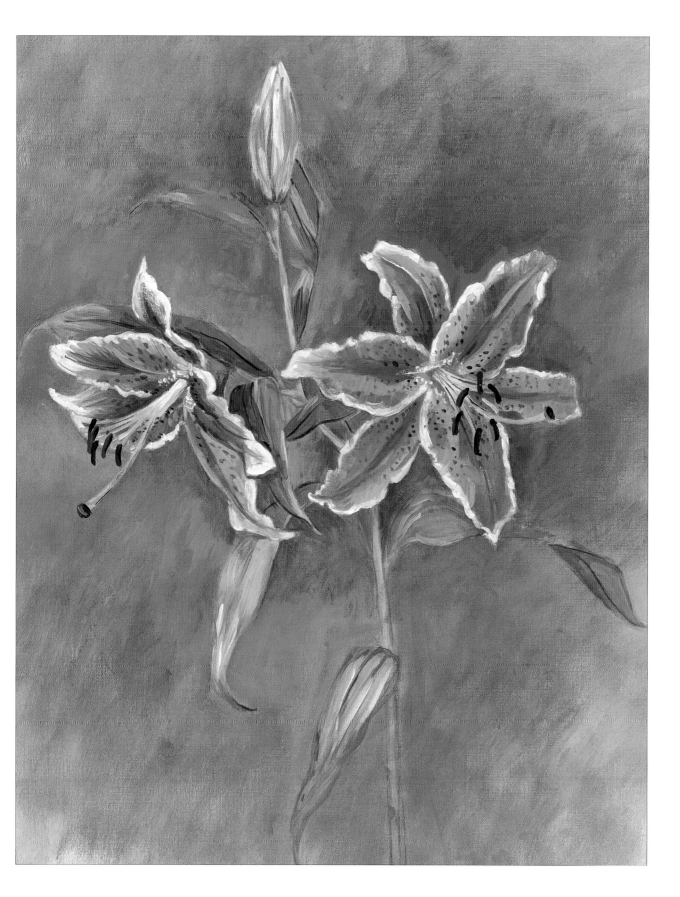

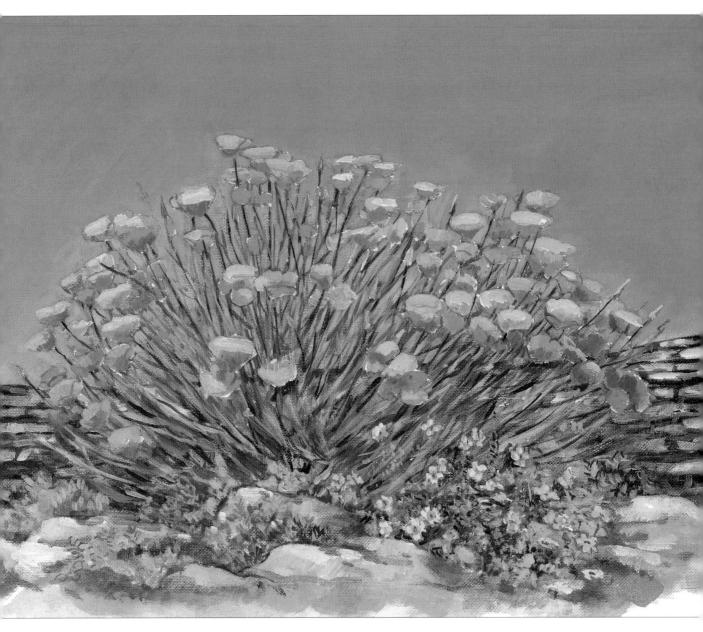

Orange on Blue
37 x 28cm (14½ x 11in)

I love the vibrant contrast between the bright orange poppies and the vivid blue sky – see Complementary colours, page 82. I used masking fluid to conceal the poppy heads enabling me to paint the stalks and sky. I added the strong cadmium orange and yellow after removing the masking fluid.

Opposite
Red Poppies
30 x 43cm (12 x 17in)

These flowers have quite a crinkly surface, and when the sun shines through them, the bright red petals can look orange or crimson. I added modelling paste to the paint and used a painting knife to apply thick textured layers of red, orange and crimson with a mix of purple and phthalo green for the dark centres. I put in the background foliage of warm and cool greens quite roughly using a mixture of criss-cross brush strokes and the painting knife.

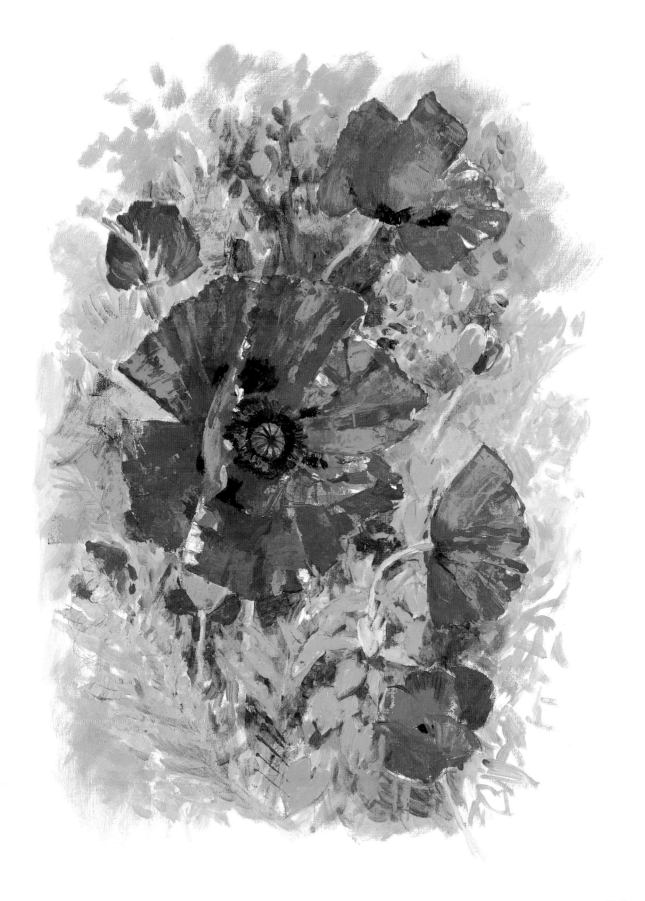

CREATIVE ACRYLIC TECHNIQUES

by Wendy Jelbert

Acrylics are perhaps the most versatile of all painting mediums – you can do virtually anything with them, which is why they are particularly favoured by the adventurous painter! Acrylics have unique characteristics, and you will enjoy them more as you get to know these special features and exploit them in your own way.

Naturally, paints and additives are fully intermixable within one brand range, but my students and I have also mixed brands together without noticing any problems.

There is an extraordinary variety of additives – texture pastes and gels, matt and gloss mediums, flow enhancers, etc. – to complement a wide range of colours. Paints, which come in small and large tubes and pots, can be thick and buttery or thin and watery. Apart from standard colours, there is a gorgeous selection of fluorescent, metallic and iridescent shades, all of which are fabulous for experimental work – so you have a real treasure trove to work with!

So, where do we start? In this section I introduce you to lots of creative techniques, then show you how to apply them using exciting step-by-step demonstrations. I have kept the projects as simple as possible; I want to encourage you to experiment and use your imagination rather than rely on a deep pocket! Mastering new techniques involves determination and lots of practice, an interaction of trial and error, taking risks with paint and materials, and some happy accidents which we all hope for in our artistic endeavours!

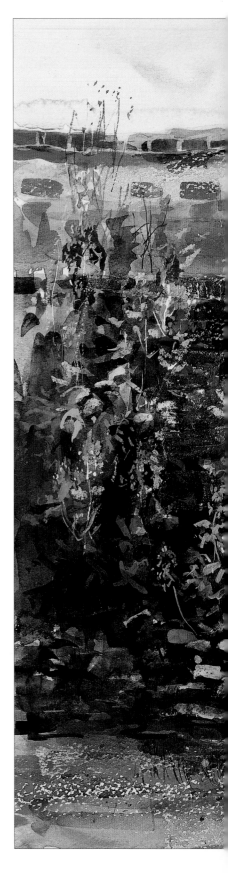

Opposite
Walled Garden
Size: 51 x 42cm (20 x 16½in)

Here I used several acrylic texture pastes and gels to enhance the weathered and aged effects on the walls, and to define the patterned bricks and stonework.

The bright foreground area and the sunlit flowers contrast with the darker tones of the wall, and entice the eye through the doorway to the garden beyond.

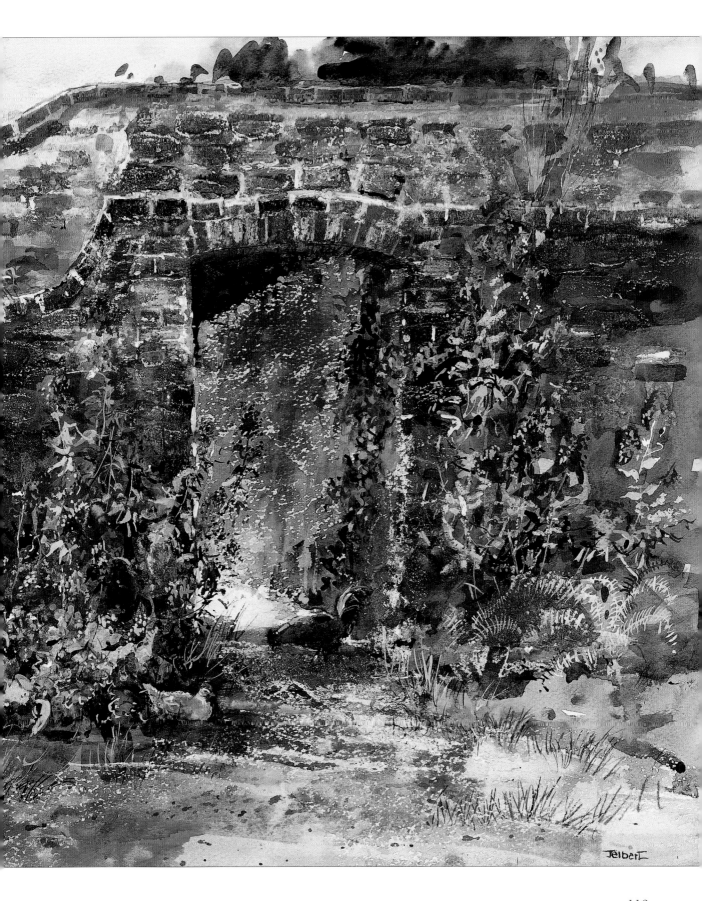

119

Creative techniques

Acrylic paints are very versatile: they can be diluted and worked to give an appearance similar to that of watercolours, or they can be applied much thicker to resemble oils. You can see some of the techniques achievable with acrylics on pages 16–19. On these pages, I show you some more techniques. This diversity of application requires practice, and care should be taken to match the method with the subject matter.

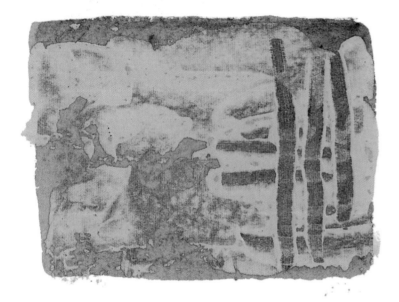

Here, I brushed a base layer of neat blue on the paper. When this was dry, I used a palette knife to apply neat yellow, leaving some quite thick and spreading other parts thinly to create blurred shapes with some of the blue showing through.

This technique is unique to acrylics, and can be used to great effect. I applied various colours to the paper; some quite thickly, others as washes, then allowed the paint to become slightly dry. I then placed the paper under running water and rubbed the surface with my fingers to wash away some of the colour. The result is an abstract, partly painted under-picture ready to be re-focused and completed.

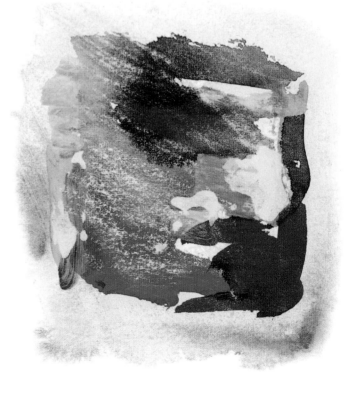

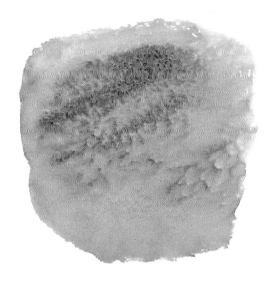

Salt can be very beguiling when used with acrylics – just as it is with watercolour washes. Having laid a wash of acrylic, I immediately sprinkled salt over it then left it to react chemically with the paint.

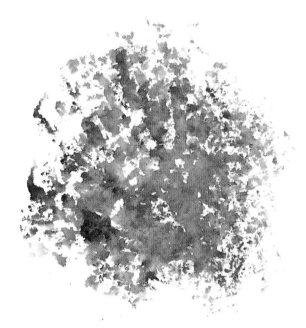

Gorgeous effects can be created with sponges. Try out several different types of sponge with various thicknesses of paint. Layers of sponged colours can add a fragile and alluring depth to subjects such as trees and shrubs.

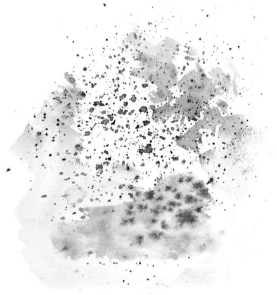

Spattering is a technique that I use to create random spots of colour. Here, I have dampened the bottom part of the paper, then spattered an acrylic wash all over. I create the spattering by drawing a loaded brush across my finger.

Creating texture

Acrylics are extremely adaptable, with a wonderful untamed quality which lends itself to the creation of texture, and this limitless potential can be both fun and challenging. There are lots of ready-made texture pastes and gels available, but you can also use materials such as plastic food wrap, PVA glue, sand, grit, eggshells, etc., to create other exciting effects.

On these pages I show you some of the materials I use to create surface textures. Try out these exercises, then explore ways of solving specific textural problems and expressing yourself in future work.

Sometimes, having created a superb patterned surface, you can conjure a painting around it. Alternatively, the subject matter may dictate a particular theme. However, do restrict yourself to a constructive plan, and try not to overwork textures. Do not keep repeating the same texture just because it works, or you will eventually produce slick and boring pictures. Keep on the move with exploratory splashing, dabbing and impasto effects and you will soon have some unexpected and fabulous results!

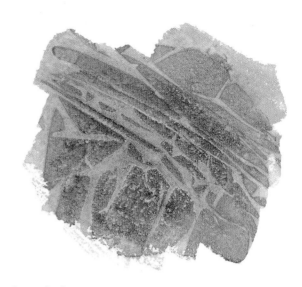

Plastic food wrap
Paint a watery but brightly coloured acrylic wash on the paper, then apply a pleated square of plastic food wrap, supporting one side with your fingers and pulling with the other across the wash, so it captures air pockets and forms patterns. Remove the food wrap when the paint is completely dry. This technique is excellent for backgrounds, foregrounds, individual flowers and leaves and many other types of textured surface.

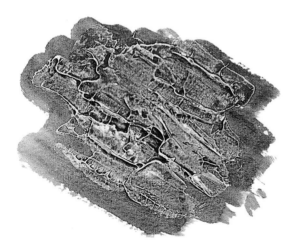

White acrylic impasto
This is one of my favourite texture techniques. Use an old brush or a palette knife and white acrylic to create an impasto study, leave it to dry, then lay wet washes over the surface, allowing some colour to become concentrated in the deep parts of the impasto. This is a superb texture for abstracts, and for weathered wooden surfaces.

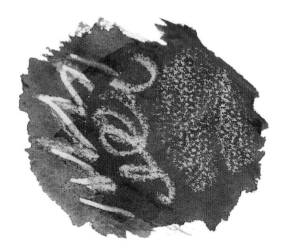

Oil pastels
Applying pale-coloured oil pastels under and over an acrylic wash can create some lovely aged and weathered effects. You should also try applying them over a dry acrylic painted surface.

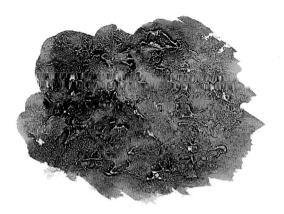

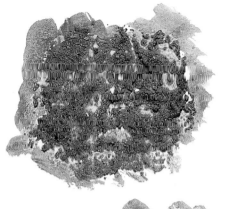

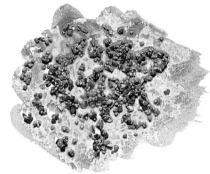

Texture pastes

There are many ready-made texture pastes and gels available for use with acrylic paints. These contain materials such as glass beads, fibres and fine, medium and coarse black grit, and you should experiment with these at your leisure. Apply the paste to the surface, leave it to dry, then paint over the top. This is an example of a coarse sand texture paste, roughened in places to create a rocky effect.

Sand and grit on texture paste

Apply a layer of fine texture paste or gel, or an acrylic medium, on the paper, then sprinkle fine sand or grit on top. Let this dry, then use an old brush to paint over the textured surface; working colour into the open spaces and leaving some of the natural colour of the sand or grit to shine through. The resultant textures are excellent for seaside studies, old walls, gritty footpaths and even some types of foliage. For these two examples, I used fine sand (top) and budgerigar grit, which contains no impurities.

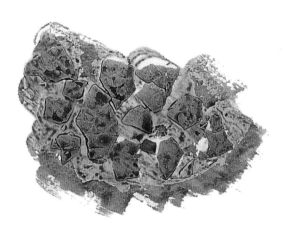

Collage textures

PVA glue can be used to secure found objects – small gems, coloured papers, pencil shavings, eggshells, etc – on to bare paper to build up collages and some fantastic effects. Acrylic paints and texture pastes also have an amazing adhesive quality and many found objects can be pressed into these. For this example, I used pieces of broken eggshells to create the stone blocks of an old wall, then painted colour over the top. You may need to place a weight (a jam jar full of water) on top of the found objects to hold them in position until the glue is thoroughly dry.

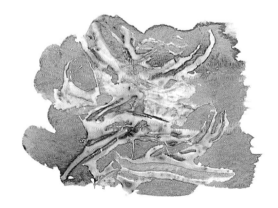

PVA glue

Dribble and swirl PVA glue on the surface of the paper, leave it to dry, then run a wash over the raised surface. This technique can be used to good effect to depict swirling water.

Applying techniques

Having practised the exercises on the previous pages, start to work up small studies such as these. Applying texture techniques effectively involves careful study of the chosen subject and a little imagination. Be prepared to take risks, and you may be surprised at what you can achieve.

Sympathy with the chosen subject is also important, and is one of the factors that make up a successful painting. Choosing an additional ingredient is rather like getting a recipe in cooking correctly proportioned!

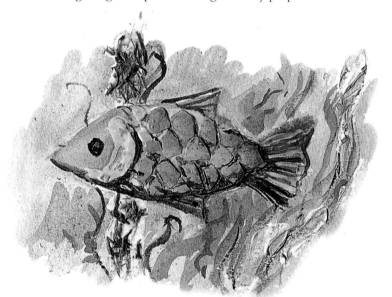

The textures on this fish were created using eggshells, tissue paper, a smooth gel (used as an adhesive), and thick white acrylic paint. I started by outlining the fish with a simple background wash. The eggshells were broken into fish scale shapes then these were stuck down with the smooth gel. White acrylic paint, straight from the tube, was applied with a palette knife to create the weeds at the right-hand side. I crushed some tissue paper into tight folds, then glued this behind the fish's head. I let everything dry thoroughly, then completed the painting using mixes of yellow ochre, cerulean blue and burnt sienna.

This simple seascape, with its dominant rough wave and distant lighthouse, shows the wonderful effects that can be achieved with salt. Apply the salt crystals to wet washes, then watch the chemical reaction take place before your eyes. The results are unpredictable, but you can stop the reaction at any time by drying the paper with a hairdryer. However, do not hold the hairdryer too close to the paper or you will blow the salt away.

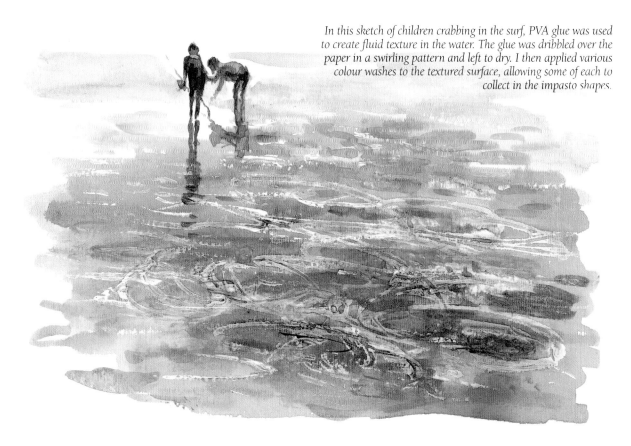

In this sketch of children crabbing in the surf, PVA glue was used to create fluid texture in the water. The glue was dribbled over the paper in a swirling pattern and left to dry. I then applied various colour washes to the textured surface, allowing some of each to collect in the impasto shapes.

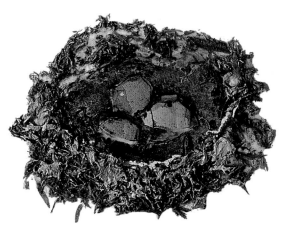

This study is a collage of bits and pieces. I used PVA glue as the base, then pushed in pencil shavings to form the nest shape and broken eggshells for the eggs.

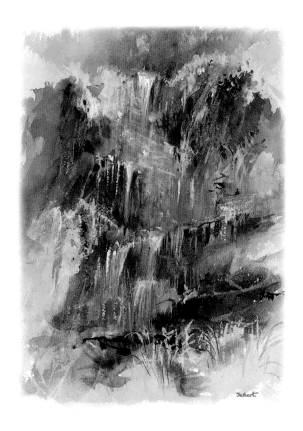

Masking fluid, applied with a ruling pen and an old brush, was used to create the highlights in this waterfall study. I then used thin, watercolour-like washes for the background and thicker paint, applied with both brush and palette knife, for the jagged rocks. This study also involved the mixing greens which is always an exciting challenge.

Lilac Blooms

I love painting flowers and lilac is one of my favourite subjects. The mass of purple-blue, star-shaped florets creates a wonderful texture and the weighty blooms arch to form interesting shapes. I have therefore chosen lilac as my first subject. This demonstration was painted on a 265 x 370mm (10½ x 14½in) sheet of 300gsm (140lb) Not surface paper. It combines several techniques: laying plastic food wrap on wet washes to create an interesting background; applying masking fluid to create highlights; working wet into wet to develop subtle blended colours; and sponging thick paint to create a random impasto texture.

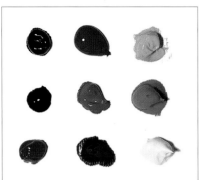

Colours:

Dark olive green, light olive green, cadmium yellow, phthalo blue, cerulean blue, light blue violet, fluorescent pink, burnt sienna and titanium white.

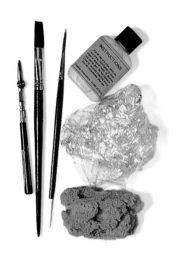

Materials:

Ruling pen, No. 8 flat brush, rigger brush, masking fluid, plastic food wrap, sponge.

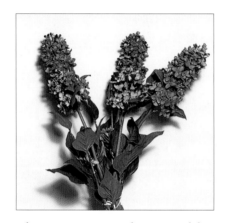

Lilac was not in season when I painted this demonstration, so I used a few silk blooms for reference.

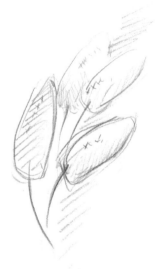

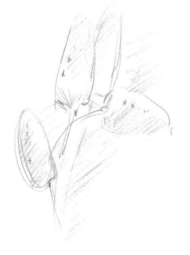

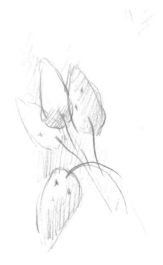

I find it useful to make detail sketches of various arrangements before making a tonal sketch of the final composition.

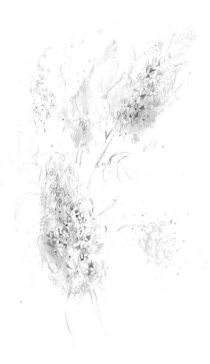

Having decided on my composition, I made this tonal sketch as the final reference. I love drawing with aquarelle pencils and here I used a blue one. I sketched the background shapes in light soft tones, then used deeper ones to define the shapes of the foreground blooms and to add the details of the leaves and star-shaped florets.

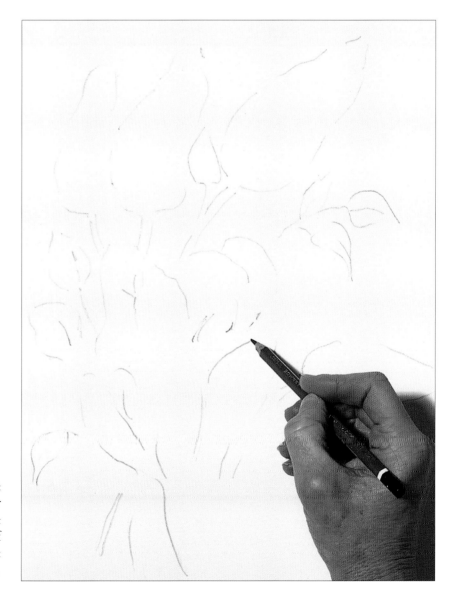

1 Transfer the outlines of the composition on to the watercolour paper. I normally use an aquarelle pencil, toned to suit the colours of the painting, but for photographic purposes I have used a B pencil.

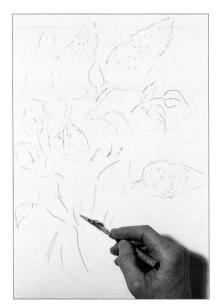

2. Use the ruling pen and masking fluid to mask out the florets on the flower heads, and the highlights and veins on the leaves. Leave to dry.

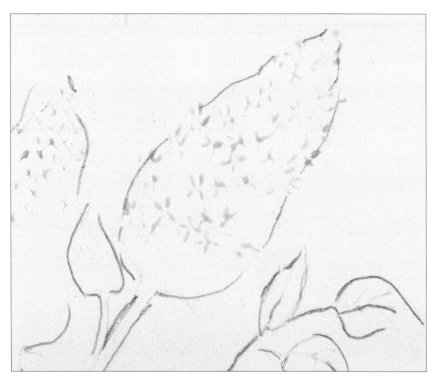

Close up of the masking fluid applied to the flower heads in step 2.

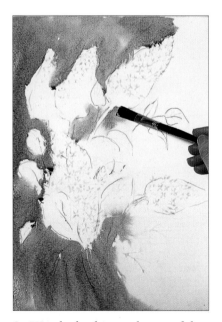

3. Wet the background areas of the paper then lay in a wash of dark olive green mixed with a touch of phthalo blue. Work down the left-hand side first.

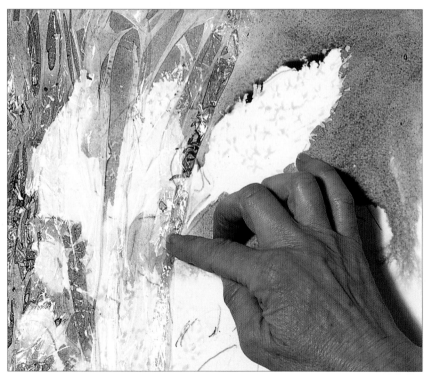

4. Arrange lengths of plastic food wrap on top of the wet paint, then scrunch it slightly to form random patterns.

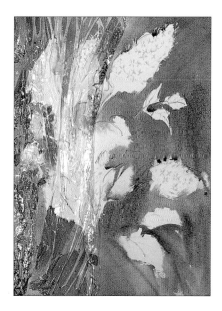

5. Use tones of the previous green mix to paint the rest of the background, then, working wet into wet, drop in a mix of light olive green and cadmium yellow with a touch of burnt sienna.

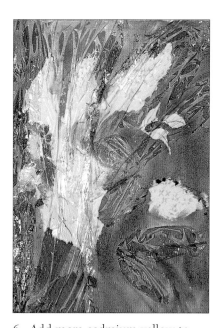

6. Add more cadmium yellow to the pale green mix, then paint the leaves. Place a piece of plastic food wrap on the top right-hand corner of the painting, then add small pieces on the wet leaves.

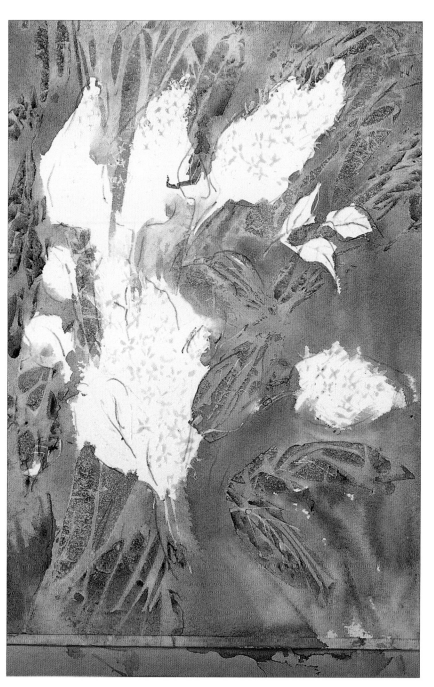

7. Leave the painting to dry, then carefully remove the plastic food wrap. You can speed up the drying process with a hairdryer, but take care not to disturb the plastic food wrap; operate the hairdryer on a low speed setting and hold it well away from the surface of the painting.

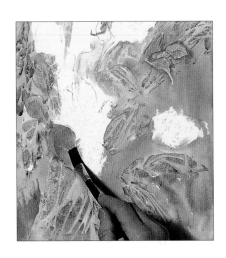

8. Mix cadmium yellow with touches of burnt sienna and light olive green, then paint the other leaves in the composition; create darker areas by adding more green to the mix.

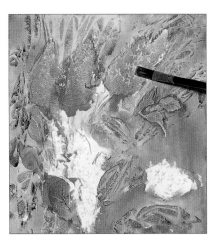

9. Wet the flower heads with clean water, then lay in a wash of light blue violet mixed with cerulean blue. Darken the bottom of each flower head.

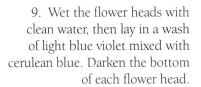

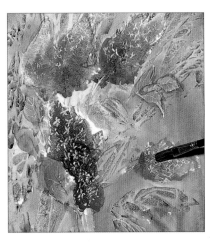

10. Working wet into wet, drop in patches of light blue violet mixed with fluorescent pink. Add touches of cerulean blue at the top of each flower head. Darken the pink mix with phthalo blue, then drop this into the lower parts of the flower heads.

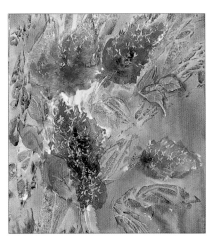

11. Continue applying touches of all the blue mixes to create shape and form.

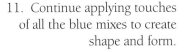

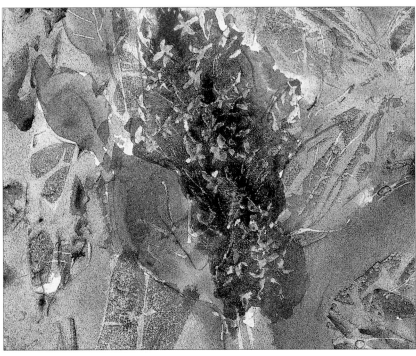

Close up of the bottom flower head showing the subtle shades of blue and pink created in steps 10 and 11.

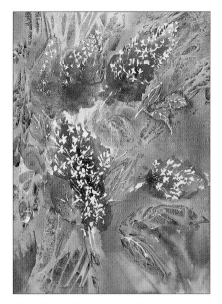

12. Carefully remove all the masking fluid.

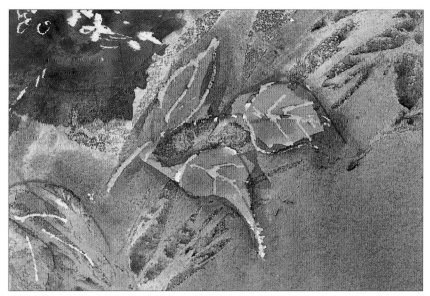

13. Mix a weak, pale green wash (cadmium yellow with pale olive green) then block in the leaves to give tone to their veins. Paint in the leaf between the top flower heads and the one at bottom left.

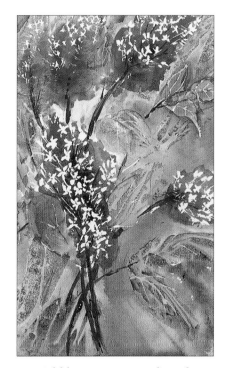

14. Add burnt sienna to the pale green mix, then paint the flower stems. Add touches of this colour to the flower heads to denote the branch structure for the florets in the flower heads.

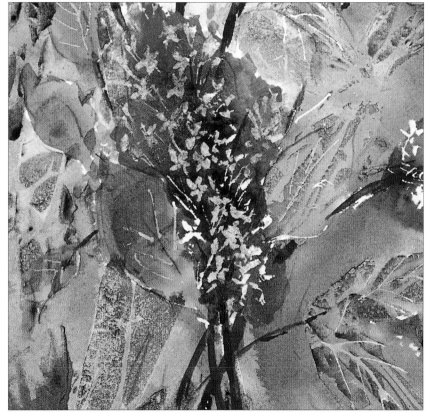

15. Use weak washes of the blue and pink mixes to soften the highlights left by the removal of the masking fluid.

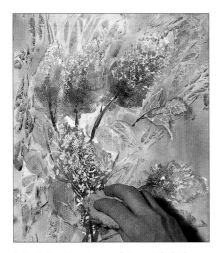

16. Mix titanium white with light blue violet, neat and thick, then use a sponge to dab highlights at the top of the flower heads. Make a slightly wetter mix of phthalo blue and fluorescent pink then dab this on the bottom part of each flower head.

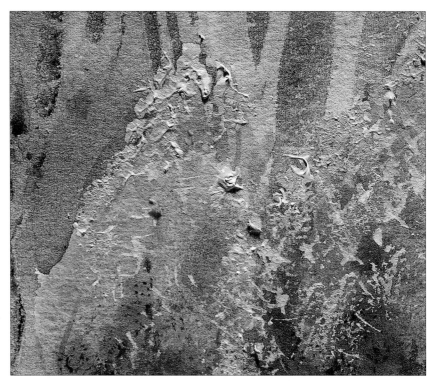

Close up of the top of a flower head showing the sponged texture applied in step 16.

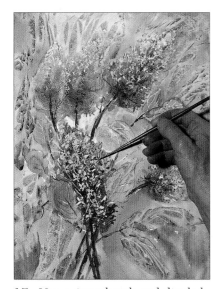

17. Use a rigger brush and the dark blue mix to paint the centre of the florets and buds, to draw in the shapes of the petals of the florets, to create shadows on the stems and to add 'negative' darks that give depth and shape to the flower heads.

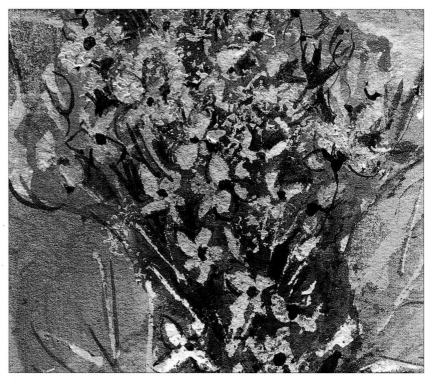

Close up of the bottom flower head showing the details applied in step 17.

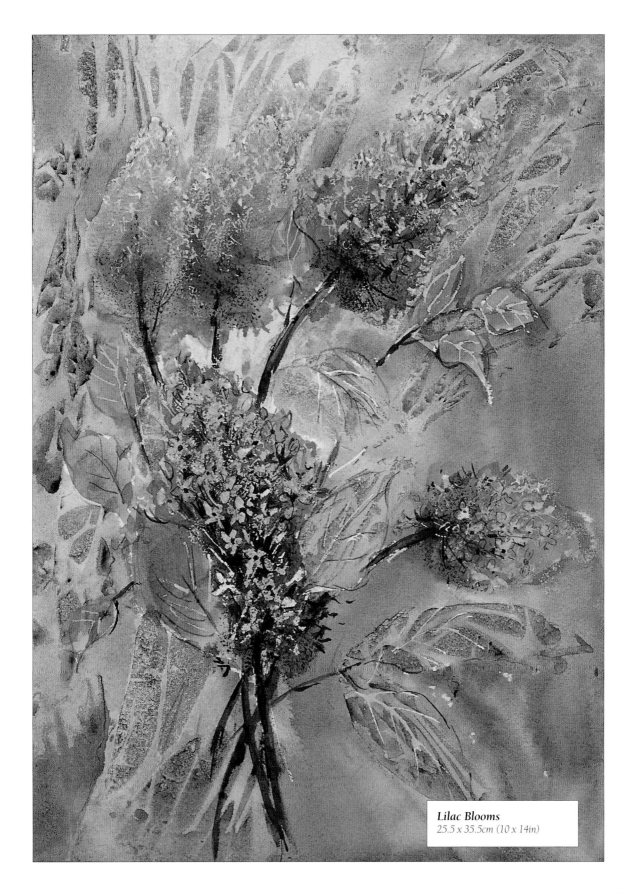

Lilac Blooms
25.5 x 35.5cm (10 x 14in)

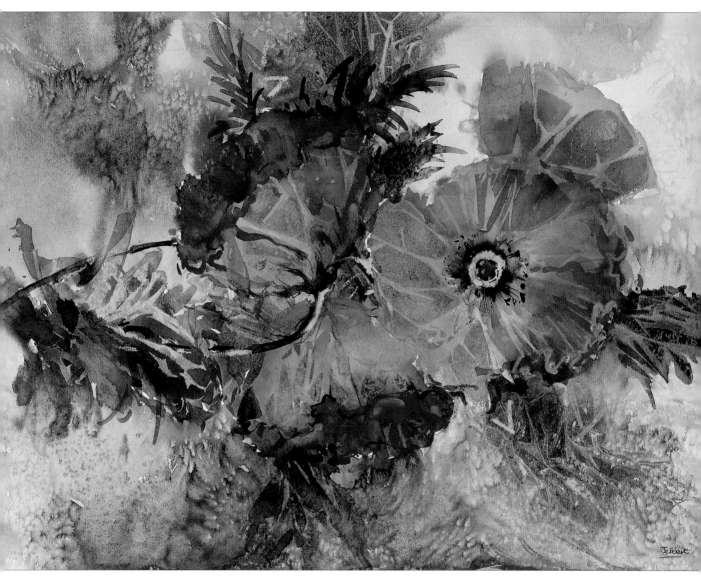

Poppies
51 x 38cm (20 x 15in)

Poppies are probably the most popular of all flower subjects, but here I have used plastic food wrap to create a completely different interpretation. Experimenting with acrylic techniques is well worth the effort – and often produces unexpected and surprising results.

Opposite
Lilies
25.5 x 35.5cm (10 x 14in)

The amazing effects of using plastic food wrap on acrylic watery washes can be adapted for both flowers and their backgrounds. Here I have used separate strips and squares to create the abstract patterns, petals and leaves. Masking fluid may also be added to the initial drawing for details such as the stamens and stalks. Remember that, when completing the picture, you can always alter the patterns by painting over them.

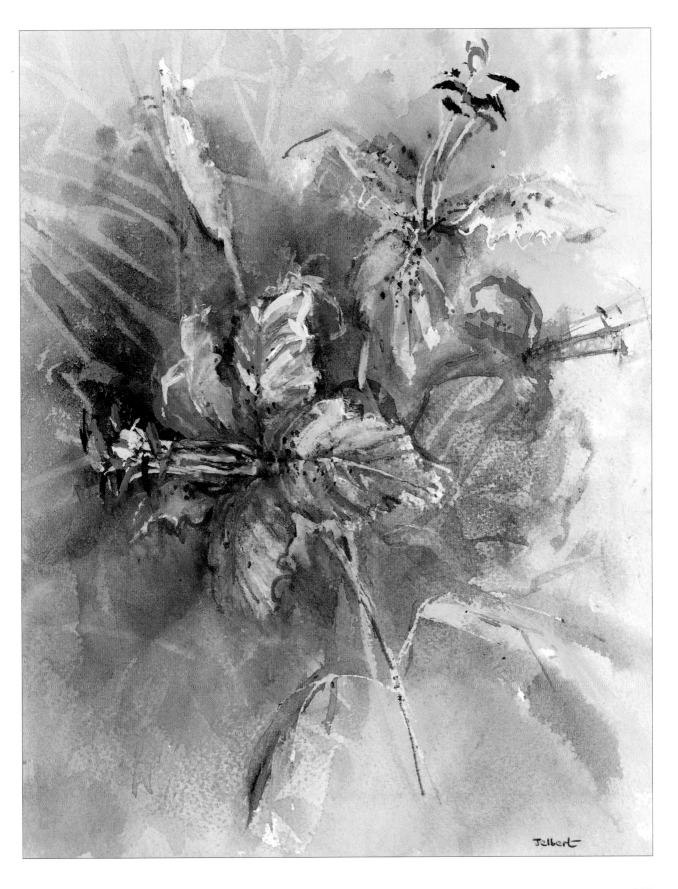

135

Seascape

I decided to include a seascape as my final demonstration because water and rocks provide an abundant source of textures, shapes, tones and colours. This composition, which includes swirling water, crashing waves and spray-soaked rocks, allows me to combine brush and palette knife work with masking fluid, texture pastes, PVA glue and acrylics in one painting.
I painted this demonstration on a 405 x 305mm (16 x 12in) sheet of 300gsm (140lb) Not surface paper.

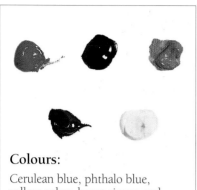

Colours:

Cerulean blue, phthalo blue, yellow ochre, burnt sienna and titanium white. You will also need dioxazine violet.

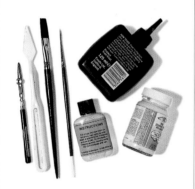

Materials:

Ruling pen, palette knife, No. 8 flat brush, rigger brush, PVA glue, masking fluid, texture paste.

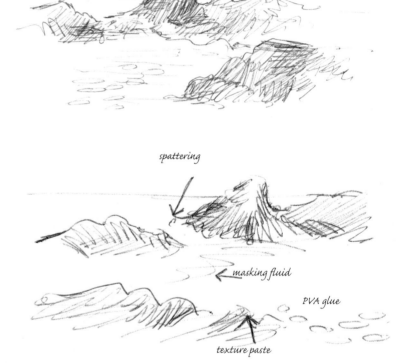

spattering

masking fluid

PVA glue

texture paste

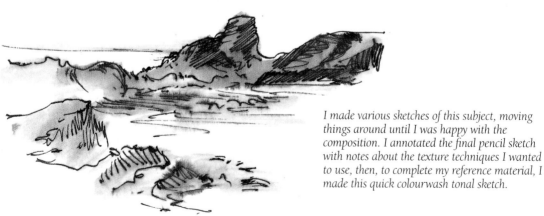

I made various sketches of this subject, moving things around until I was happy with the composition. I annotated the final pencil sketch with notes about the texture techniques I wanted to use, then, to complete my reference material, I made this quick colourwash tonal sketch.

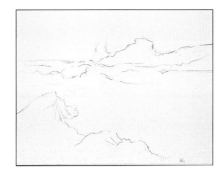

1. Sketch the basic outlines of the final composition on to the watercolour paper.

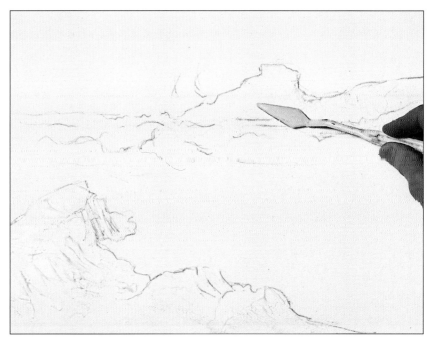

2. Use a palette knife to apply texture paste quite thickly to the foreground rocks, and slightly less thickly on the distant ones.

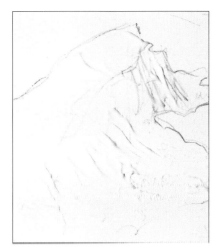

Close up showing the texture paste applied to the foreground in step 2.

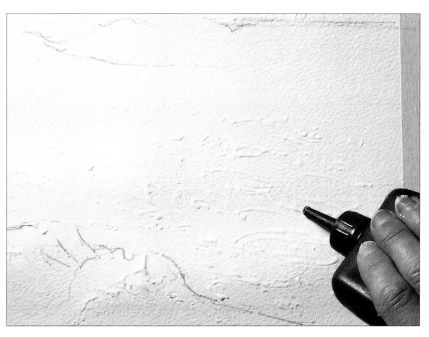

3. Working from the nozzle on the bottle of PVA glue, apply swirls of glue across the foreground area of the sea.

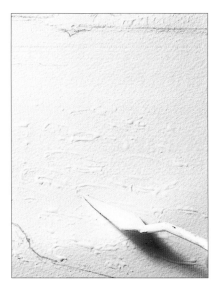

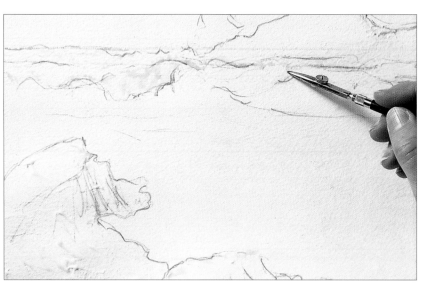

4. Use the tip of the palette knife to move the PVA glue into finer swirls. Leave to dry.

5. Use the ruling pen to apply masking fluid to the top of the breaking wave and along the tops of the distant rocks.

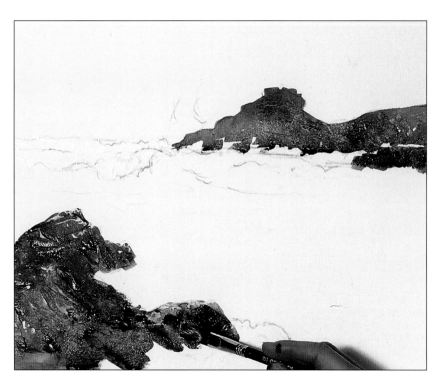

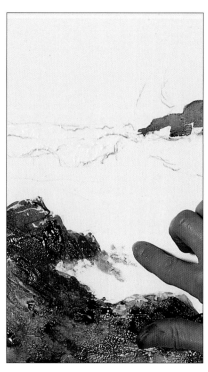

6. Mix burnt sienna with a touch of dioxazine violet, then block in the rocks in the distance and those in the foreground. Add a touch of phthalo blue to the mix in the foreground. Use bold random strokes to create shape and form. Leave some speckles of white paper.

7. Use your finger to soften the hard edges of the rocks where they meet the water, then leave the paint to dry slightly.

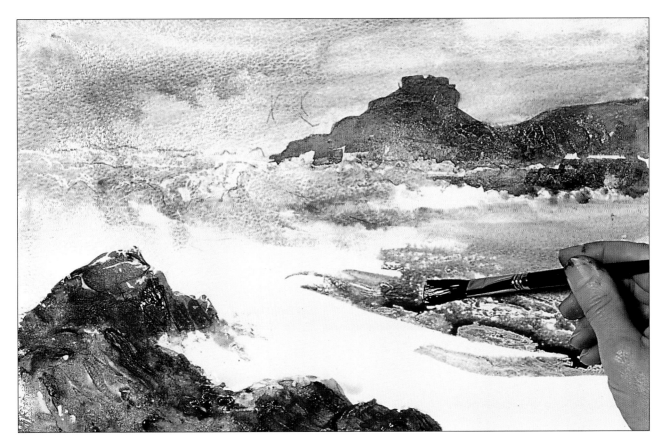

8. While the rocks are still damp, wet the rest of the white paper, then use a wash of cerulean blue with a touch of burnt sienna to paint the sky. Mix a wash of phthalo blue with touches of cerulean blue and burnt sienna and paint the sea.

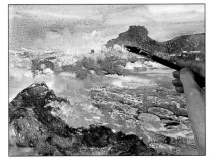

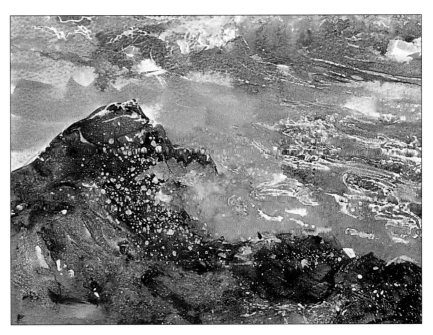

9. Use tones of the two blues to build up shape and form in the sky and sea. Spatter titanium white to create spray on the distant headland.

10. Use the same mix to spatter foam on the foreground rocks.

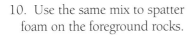

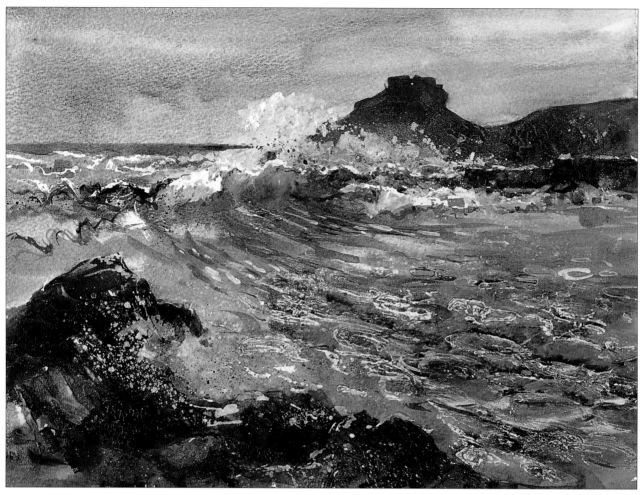

The finished painting
Size: 36 x 26cm (14¼ x 10¼in)

I removed the masking fluid, then used a rigger brush to add dark accents of colour to develop shape and form. I used the dark blue mix to emphasise the large wave in the centre of the painting. I spattered some darks on the breaking waves to create a contrast with the white spray. Finally, I softened some of the white area exposed by removing the masking fluid with a weak wash of yellow ochre.

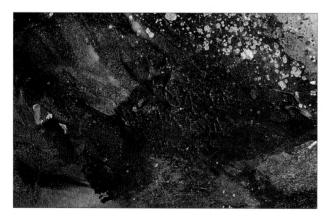

Close up of the foreground showing the effect of texture paste.

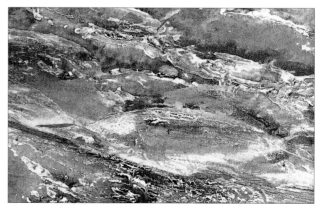

Close up of foreground sea showing the effect of PVA glue.

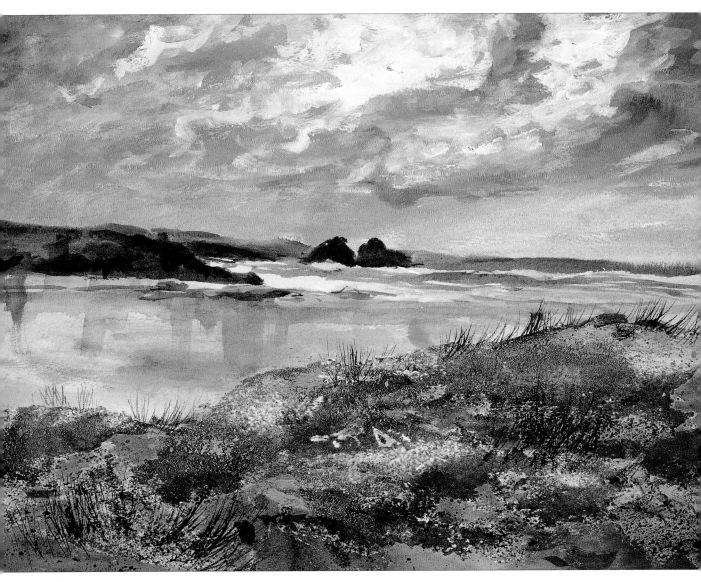

Low Tide
Size: 46 x 33cm (18 x 13in)

This heavily textured foreground was built up with a gritty texture paste and an apricot undercoat was applied all over the paper. The painting was then rendered with a combination of thick paint applied with a palette knife and watery washes applied with a brush.

The Boat Race
Size: 51 x 40.5cm (20 x 16in)

This composition uses scale, texture and detail to impart a dramatic sense of space and distance. The foreground grasses are large and the sandy areas are heavily textured. The figures in the middle distance, which are relatively smaller and less detailed, give the viewer a general idea of scale. Then, in the far distance, the boats are defined by simple triangular marks set at interesting angles against the far shoreline.

I started this painting by using a rag to rub an orange undercoat across all the paper. I used acrylics as oils to paint in the sky, then the wet-into-wet technique to create the soft distant headland. In the foreground, I applied thick paint with a palette knife to add light and sparkle to the dunes.

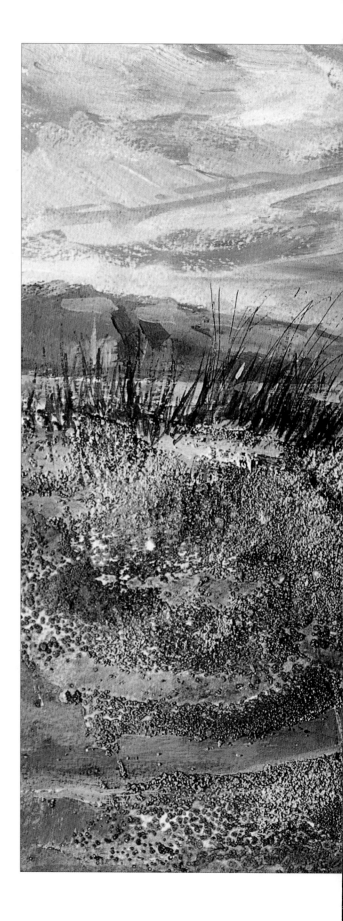

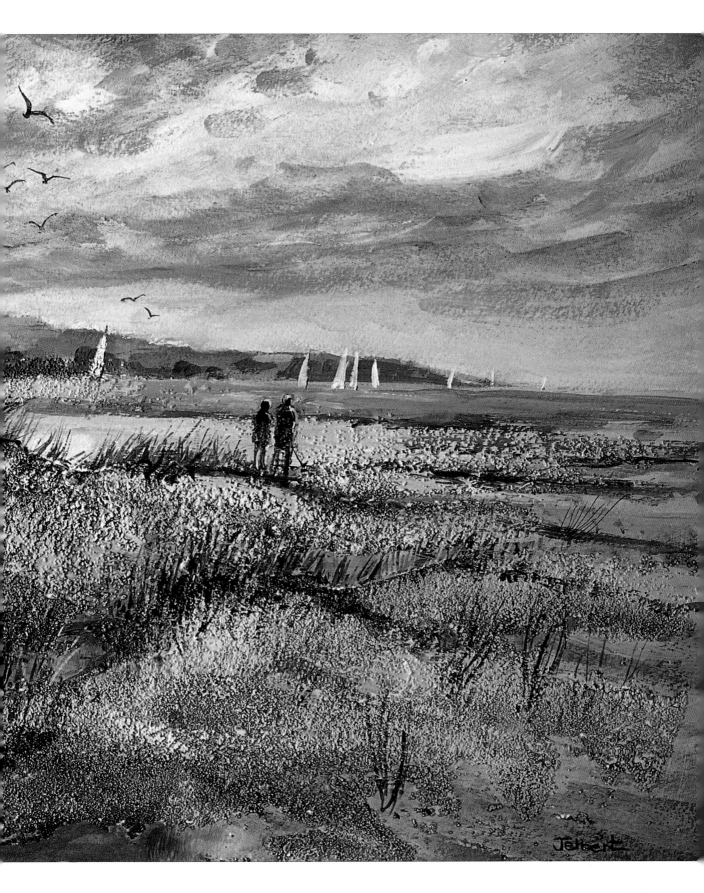

Index

Rocky Coastline by Wendy Jelbert
33 x 21.5cm (13 x 8½in)

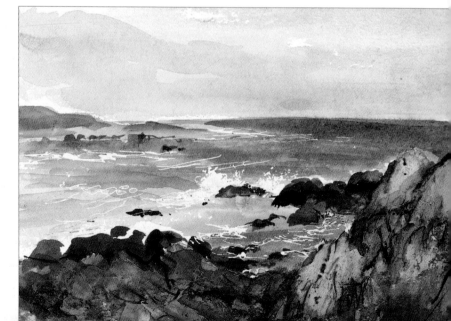